BOOK OF
GREEK
MYTHS

INGRI and EDGAR PARIN D'AULAIRE'S

BOOK OF GREEK MYTHS

DOUBLEDAY & COMPANY, INC.

GARDEN CITY, NEW YORK

Other books by Ingri and Edgar Parin d'Aulaire

ABRAHAM LINCOLN

ANIMALS EVERYWHERE

BENJAMIN FRANKLIN

BUFFALO BILL

COLUMBUS

D'AULAIRES' TROLLS

DON'T COUNT YOUR CHICKS

FOXIE

GEORGE WASHINGTON

NORSE GODS AND GIANTS

OLA

POCAHONTAS

THE TERRIBLE TROLL BIRD

ISBN: 0-385-15787-8

CONTENTS

IN OLDEN TIMES,

when men still worshiped ugly idols, there lived in the land of Greece a folk of shepherds and herdsmen who cherished light and beauty. They did not worship dark idols like their neighbors, but created instead their own beautiful, radiant gods.

The Greek gods looked much like people and acted like them, too, only they were taller; handsomer and could do no wrong. Fire-breathing monsters and beasts with many heads stood for all that was dark and wicked. They were for gods and great heroes to conquer.

The gods lived on top of Olympus, a mountain so high and steep that no man could climb it and see them in their shining palace. But they often descended to earth, sometimes in their own shapes, sometimes disguised as humans or animals.

Mortals worshiped the gods and the gods honored Mother Earth. They had all sprung from her, for she was the beginning of all life.

GAEA, the Earth, came out of darkness so long ago that nobody knows when or how. Earth was young and lonesome, for nothing lived on her yet. Above her rose Uranus, the Sky, dark and blue, set all over with sparkling stars. He was magnificent to behold, and young Earth looked up at him and fell in love with him. Sky smiled down at Earth, twinkling with his countless stars, and they were joined in love. Soon young Earth became Mother Earth, the mother of all things living. All her children loved their warm and bountiful mother and feared their mighty father, Uranus, lord of the universe.

THE TITANS

THE TITANS were the first children of Mother Earth. They were the first gods, taller than the mountains she created to serve them as thrones, and both Earth and Sky were proud of them. There were six Titans, six glorious gods, and they had six sisters, the Titanesses, whom they took for their wives.

When Gaea again gave birth, Uranus was not proud. Their new children were also huge, but each had only one glowing eye set in the middle of his forehead. They were the three Cyclopes and they were named Lightning, Thunder, and Thunderbolt. They were not handsome gods, but tremendously strong smiths. Sparks from their heavy hammers flashed across the sky and lit up the heavens so brightly that even their father's stars faded.

After a while Mother Earth bore three more sons. Uranus looked at them with disgust. Each of them had fifty heads and a hundred strong arms. He hated to see such ugly creatures walk about on lovely Earth, so he seized them and their brothers the Cyclopes and flung them into Tartarus, the deepest, darkest pit under the earth.

Mother Earth loved her children and could not forgive her husband for his cruelty to them. Out of hardest flint she fashioned a sickle and spoke to her sons the Titans:

"Take this weapon, make an end to your father's cruelty and set your brothers free."

Fear took hold of five of the Titans and they trembled and refused. Only Cronus, the youngest but the strongest, dared to take the sickle. He fell upon his father. Uranus could not withstand the weapon wielded by his strong son and he fled, giving up his powers.

Mother Earth made Pontus, the boundless seas, her second husband, and from this union sprang the gods of the watery depths. And from her rich ground grew an abundance of trees and flowers and, out of her crevices, sprites, beasts, and early man crept forth.

CRONUS was now the lord of the universe. He sat on the highest mountain and ruled over heaven and earth with a firm hand. The other gods obeyed his will and early man worshiped him. This was man's Golden Age. Men lived happily and in peace with the gods and each other. They did not kill and they had no locks on their doors, for theft had not yet been invented.

But Cronus did not set his monstrous brothers free, and Mother Earth was angry with him and plotted his downfall. She had to wait, for no god yet born was strong enough to oppose him. But she knew that one of his sons would be stronger than he, just as Cronus had been stronger than his father. Cronus knew it too, so every time his Titaness-wife Rhea gave birth, he took the newborn god and swallowed it. With all of his offspring securely inside him, he had nothing to fear.

14

But Rhea mourned. Her five sisters, who had married the five other Titans, were surrounded by their Titan children, while she was all alone. When Rhea expected her sixth child, she asked Mother Earth to help her save the child from his father. That was just what Mother Earth had been waiting for. She gave her daughter whispered advice, and Rhea went away smiling.

As soon as Rhea had borne her child, the god Zeus, she hid him. Then she wrapped a stone in baby clothes and gave it to her husband to swallow instead of her son. Cronus was fooled and swallowed the stone, and the little god Zeus was spirited away to a secret cave on the island of Crete. Old Cronus never heard the cries of his young son, for Mother Earth set noisy earth sprites outside the cave. They made such a clatter, beating their shields with their swords, that other sounds were drowned out.

ZEUS
AND HIS FAMILY

ZEUS was tended by gentle nymphs and was nursed by the fairy goat Amaltheia. From the horns of the goat flowed ambrosia and nectar, the food and drink of the gods. Zeus grew rapidly, and it was not long before he strode out of the cave as a great new god. To thank the nymphs for tending him so well, he gave them the horns of the goat. They were horns of plenty and could never be emptied. From the hide of the goat he made for himself an impenetrable breastplate, the Aegis, and now he was so strong that Cronus could do nothing against him.

Young Zeus chose Metis, a Titan's daughter, for his first wife. She was the goddess of prudence, and he needed her good advice. She warned him not to try alone to overthrow his child-devouring father, for Cronus had all the other Titans and their sons on his side. First Zeus must also have strong allies.

16

Metis went to Cronus and cunningly tricked him into eating a magic herb. He thought that the herb would make him unconquerable. Instead it made him so sick that he vomited up not only the stone he had swallowed, but his five other children as well. They were the gods Hades and Poseidon and the goddesses Hestia, Demeter, and Hera, all mighty gods who right away joined forces with Zeus. When Cronus saw the six young gods rising against him, he knew that his hour had come and he surrendered his powers and fled.

Now Zeus was the lord of the universe. He did not want to rule alone. He shared his powers with his brothers and sisters. But the Titans and their sons revolted. They refused to let themselves be ruled by the new gods. Only Prometheus and his brother Epimetheus left the Titans to join Zeus, for Prometheus could look into the future and he knew that Zeus would win.

Zeus freed the monstrous sons of Mother Earth from Tartarus. Gratefully the hundred-armed ones fought for him with all their strength, and the Cyclopes forged mighty weapons for him and his brothers.

They made a trident for Poseidon. It was so forceful that when he struck the ground with it, the earth shook, and when he struck the sea, frothing waves stood mountain high.

For Hades they made a cap of invisibility so he could strike his enemies unseen, and for Zeus they forged lightning bolts. Armed with them, he was the mightiest god of them all, nothing could stand against him and his thunderbolts. The Titans fought a bitter battle, but at last they had to surrender, and Zeus locked them up in Tartarus. The hundred-armed monsters went to stand guard at the gates to see that they never escaped. Atlas, the strongest of the Titans, was sent to the end of the world to carry forever the vault of the sky on his shoulders.

Angry with Zeus for sending her sons the Titans into the dark pit of Tartarus, Mother Earth now brought forth two terrible monsters, Typhon and his mate, Echidna, and sent them against Zeus. They were so fearful that when the gods saw them they changed themselves into animals and fled in terror. Typhon's hundred horrible heads touched the stars, venom dripped from his evil eyes, and lava and red-hot stones poured from his gaping mouths. Hissing like a hundred snakes and roaring like a hundred lions, he tore up whole mountains and threw them at the gods.

Zeus soon regained his courage and turned, and when the other gods saw him taking his stand, they came back to help him fight the monster. A terrible battle raged, and hardly a living creature was left on earth. But Zeus was fated to win, and as Typhon tore up huge Mount Aetna to hurl at the gods, Zeus struck it with a hundred well-aimed thunderbolts and the mountain fell back, pinning Typhon underneath. There the monster lies to this very day, belching fire, lava, and smoke through the top of the mountain.

Echidna, his hideous mate, escaped destruction. She cowered in a cave, protecting Typhon's dreadful offspring, and Zeus let them live as a challenge to future heroes.

Now at last Mother Earth gave up her struggle. There were no more upheavals, and the wounds of the war soon healed. The mountains stood firmly anchored. The seas had their shores. The rivers had their river-beds and oxhorned river-gods watched over them, and each tree and each spring had its nymph. The earth again was green and fruitful and Zeus could begin to rule in peace.

The one-eyed Cyclopes were not only smiths but masons as well, and they built a towering palace for the gods on top of Mount Olympus, the highest mountain in Greece. The palace was hidden in clouds, and the goddesses of the seasons rolled them away whenever a god wanted to go down to earth. Nobody else could pass through the gate of clouds.

Iris, the fleet-footed messenger of the gods, had her own path down to earth. Dressed in a gown of iridescent drops, she ran along the rainbow on her busy errands between Olympus and earth.

In the gleaming hall of the palace, where light never failed, the Olympian gods sat on twelve golden thrones and reigned over heaven and earth. There were twelve great gods, for Zeus shared his powers, not only with his brothers and sisters, but with six of his children and the goddess of love as well.

Zeus himself sat on the highest throne, with a bucketful of thunderbolts beside him. On his right sat his youngest sister, Hera, whom he had chosen from all his wives as his queen. Beside her sat her son, Ares, god of war, and Hephaestus, god of fire, with Aphrodite, goddess of love, between them. Next was Zeus's son Hermes, the herald of the gods, and Zeus's sister Demeter, goddess of the harvest with her daughter, Persephone, on her lap. On the left of Zeus sat his brother Poseidon, the lord of the sea. Next to him sat the four children of Zeus: Athena, the twins Apollo and Artemis, and Dionysus, the youngest of the gods. Athena was

the goddess of wisdom, Apollo, the god of light and music, Artemis, goddess of the hunt, and Dionysus, the god of wine.

Hestia, the eldest sister of Zeus, was goddess of the hearth. She had no throne, but tended the sacred fire in the hall, and every hearth on earth was her altar. She was the gentlest of all the Olympians.

Hades, the eldest brother of Zeus, was the lord of the dead. He preferred to stay in his gloomy palace in the underworld and never went to Olympus.

The gods themselves could not die, for divine ichor flowed in their veins instead of blood. Most of the time they lived happily together, feasting on sweet-smelling ambrosia and nectar, but when their wills clashed, there were violent quarrels. Then Zeus would reach for a thunderbolt and the Olympians would tremble and fall to order, for Zeus alone was stronger than all the other gods together.

23

HERA, the beautiful queen of Olympus, was a very jealous wife. Even Zeus, who was afraid of nothing, feared her fits of temper. She hated all his other wives, and when Zeus first asked her to be his wife, she refused. Slyly Zeus created a thunderstorm, changed himself into a little cuckoo, and, pretending to be in distress, he flew into Hera's arms for protection. She pitied the wet little bird and hugged it close to keep it warm, but all of a sudden she found herself holding mighty Zeus in her arms instead of the bird.

Thus Zeus won Hera and all nature burst into bloom for their wedding. Mother Earth gave the bride a little apple tree that bore golden apples of immortality. Hera treasured the tree and planted it in the garden of the Hesperides, her secret garden far to the west. She put a hundred-headed dragon under the tree to guard the apples and ordered the three Nymphs of the Hesperides to water and care for the tree.

Zeus loved Hera dearly, but he was also very fond of rocky Greece. He often sneaked down to earth in disguise to marry mortal girls. The more wives he had, the more children he would have, and all the better for Greece! All his children would inherit some of his greatness and become great heroes and rulers. But Hera in her jealous rage tormented his other wives and children, and even Zeus was powerless to stop her. She knew how tricky Zeus could be and kept very close watch over him.

One day as Hera looked down on earth, she spied a small dark thundercloud where no cloud should have been. She rushed down and darted into the cloud. Zeus was there just as she had suspected, but with him was only a little snow-white cow. He had seen Hera coming and, to protect his newest bride Io from her wrath, he had changed the girl into a cow. Alas! The cow was as lovely as the girl, and Hera was not deceived, but she pretended to suspect nothing and begged Zeus to let her have the dainty cow. Zeus could not well refuse his queen such a little wish without giving himself away, and he had to give her the cow. Hera tied poor Io to a tree and sent her servant Argus to keep watch over her.

Argus had a hundred bright eyes placed all over his body. He was so big and strong that singlehandedly he had made an end to the monstrous Echidna, who had lived in a cave and had devoured all who passed by. He was Hera's faithful servant and the best of watchmen, for he never closed more than half of his eyes in sleep at a time.

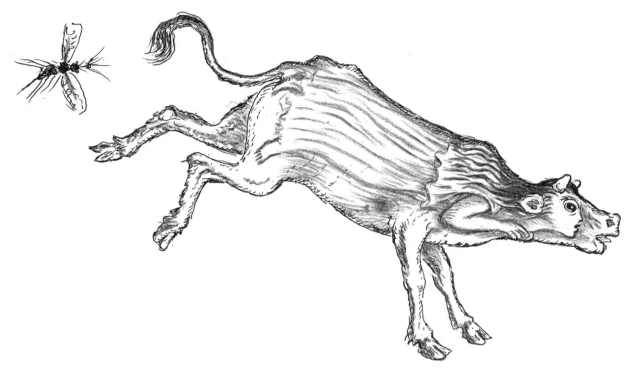

Argus sat down next to the cow and watched her with all his eyes, and poor Io had to walk on four legs and eat grass. She raised her mournful eyes to Olympus, but Zeus was so afraid of Hera that he did not dare to help her. At last he could no longer bear to see her distress, and he asked his son Hermes, the craftiest of the gods, to run down to earth and set Io free.

Hermes disguised himself as a shepherd and walked up to Argus playing a tune on his shepherd's pipe. Argus was bored, having nothing to do with all his eyes but watch a little cow, and he was glad to have music and company. Hermes sat down beside him, and after he had played for a while, he began to tell a long and dull story. It had no beginning and it had no end and fifty of Argus's eyes closed in sleep. Hermes droned on and on and slowly the fifty other eyes fell shut, one by one. Quickly Hermes touched all the eyes with his magic wand and closed them forever in eternal sleep. Argus had been bored to death.

Hermes then untied the cow, and Io ran home to her father, the river-god Inachos. He did not recognize the cow as his daughter, and Io could not tell him what had happened, all she could say was, "Mooo!" But when she lifted up her little hoof and scratched her name, "I-O," in the river sand, her father at once understood what had happened, for he knew the ways of Zeus. Inachos rose out of his river bed and rushed off to take revenge on the mighty thunder-god. He flew at Zeus in such a rage that to save himself Zeus had to throw a thunderbolt, and ever since the bed of the river Inachos in Arcadia has been dry.

Hera was furious when she saw that Argus was dead and the cow Io had been set free. She sent a vicious gadfly to sting and chase the cow. To be sure that her faithful servant Argus would never be forgotten, she took his hundred bright eyes and put them on the tail of the peacock, her favorite bird. The eyes could no longer see, but they looked gorgeous, and that went to the peacock's little head, and made it the vainest of all animals.

Pursued by the gadfly, Io ran all over Greece. Trying to escape from its tormenting sting, she jumped across the strait that separates Europe from Asia Minor, and, ever since, it has been called the Bosporus, the "cow ford."

But still the gadfly chased her all the way to the land of Egypt. When the Egyptians saw the snow-white cow, they fell to their knees and worshiped her. She became an Egyptian goddess, and Hera now permitted Zeus to change her back to her human shape. But first he had to promise never to look at Io again.

Io lived long as the goddess-queen of Egypt, and the son she bore to Zeus became king after her. Her descendants returned to Greece as great kings and beautiful queens. Poor Io's sufferings had not all been in vain.

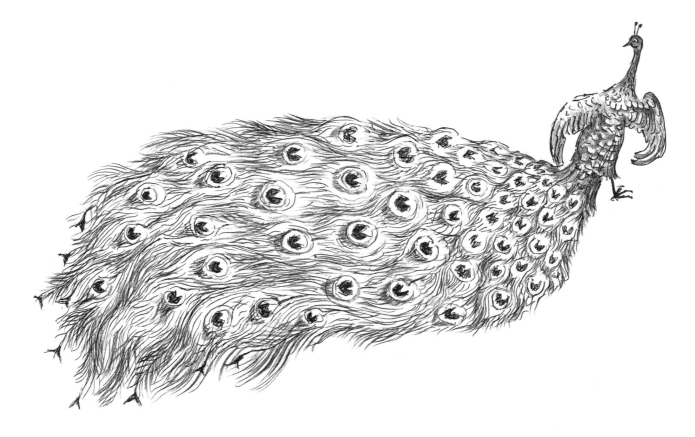

HEPHAESTUS, the god of smiths and fire, was the son of Zeus and Hera. He was a hard-working, peace-loving god and was very fond of his mother. Often he tried to soothe her temper with gentle words. Once he had even dared to step between his quarreling parents. He sided with Hera, and that made Zeus so angry that he seized his son by the legs and flung him out of Olympus. For a whole day, Hephaestus hurtled through the air. In the evening he fell on the island of Lemnos, with a thump so hard that the island shook. Thetis, a gentle sea goddess, found him all broken and bruised. She bound his wounds and nursed him back to health.

Zeus forgave him and Hephaestus returned to Olympus, but ever after, he walked like a flickering flame. His body was big and strong and his hands were wonderfully skilled, but his weak legs could not support him for long. He built for himself two robots of gold and silver to help him about. They had mechanical brains and could think for themselves. They even could speak with their tongues of silver. They also served him as helpers in his workshop on Olympus. It was there that Hephaestus made the twelve golden thrones of the gods and their marvelous weapons, chariots, and jewels.

He also had forges inside volcanoes on earth. His helpers there were the one-eyed Cyclopes. They worked his bellows and swung his heavy hammers. When Hephaestus was at work, the din of the hammers could be heard for miles and sparks flew out of the tops of the mountains.

All the Olympian gods were fond of Hephaestus and often went to his forge to admire his work. When Aphrodite, his lovely wife, came to his workshop to look at the matchless jewels he was fashioning for her, she daintly lifted her trailing garments out of the soot.

APHRODITE, the beautiful goddess of love, was the only Olympian who had neither mother nor father. Nobody knew from where she had come. The West Wind had first seen her in the pearly light of dawn as she rose out of the sea on a cushion of foam. She floated lightly over the gentle waves and was so lovely to behold that the wind almost lost his breath. With soft puffs, he blew her to the flowering island of Cythera, where the three Graces welcomed her ashore. The three Graces, goddesses of beauty, became her attendants. They dressed her in shimmering garments, bedecked her with sparkling jewels, and placed her in a golden chariot drawn by white doves. Then they led her to Olympus, where all the gods rejoiced in her beauty, seated her on a golden throne, and made her one of them.

Zeus was afraid that the gods would fight over the hand of Aphrodite, and, to prevent it, he quickly chose a husband for her. He gave her to Hephaestus, the steadiest of the gods, and he, who could hardly believe in his good luck, used all his skill to make the most lavish jewels for her. He made her a girdle of finely wrought gold and wove magic into the filigree work. That was not very wise of him, for when she wore her magic girdle no one could resist her, and she was all too irresistible already.

Aphrodite had a mischievous little son whose name was Eros. He darted about with a bow and a quiver full of arrows. They were arrows of love and he delighted in shooting them into the hearts of unwary victims. Whoever was hit by one of his arrows fell head over heels in love with the first person he saw, while Eros laughed mockingly.

Once a year Aphrodite returned to Cythera and dived into the sea from which she had come. Sparkling and young, she rose from the water, as dewy fresh as on the day when she had first been seen. She loved gaiety and glamour and was not at all pleased at being the wife of sooty, hardworking Hephaestus. She would rather have had his brother Ares for her husband.

30

ARES, god of war, was tall and handsome but vain, and as cruel as his brother Hephaestus was kind. Eris, the spirit of strife, was his constant companion. Eris was sinister and mean, and her greatest joy was to make trouble. She had a golden apple that was so bright and shiny everybody wanted to have it. When she threw it among friends, their friendship came to a rapid end. When she threw it among enemies, war broke out, for the golden apple of Eris was an apple of discord.

When Ares heard the clashing of arms, he grinned with glee, put on his gleaming helmet, and leapt into his war chariot. Brandishing his sword like a torch, he rushed into the thick of battle, not caring who won or lost as long as much blood was shed. A vicious crowd followed at his heels, carrying with them Pain, Panic, Famine, and Oblivion.

Once in a while, Ares himself was wounded. He was immortal but he could not bear to suffer pain and screamed so loudly that he could be heard for miles. Then he would run home to Olympus, where Zeus in disgust called him the worst of his children and told him to stop his howling. His wounds, treated with the ointment of the gods, quickly healed, and Ares returned as good as ever and seated himself on his throne, tall, handsome, and boastful, the plume on his golden helmet nodding proudly.

Aphrodite admired him for his splendid looks, but none of the other gods were fond of him, least of all his half sister Athena. She loathed his vain strutting and senseless bloodshed.

ATHENA, the goddess of wisdom, was the favorite child of Zeus. She had sprung fully grown out of her father's head.

Her mother was Metis, goddess of prudence, the first wife of Zeus. He depended on her, for he needed her wise council, but Mother Earth warned him that, were Metis to bear him a son, this son would dethrone him as Zeus had dethroned Cronus, his father who had dethroned his own father, Uranus. This must not happen, thought Zeus, but he could not do without her advice, so he decided to swallow her. Slyly, he proposed that they play a game of changing shapes, and Metis, forgetting her prudence, playfully turned herself into all kinds of animals, big and small. Just as she had taken on the shape of a little fly, Zeus opened wide his mouth, took a deep breath, and zip! he swallowed the fly. Ever after, Metis sat in his head and guided him from there.

Now it happened that Metis was going to have a daughter, and she sat inside Zeus's head hammering out a helmet and weaving a splendid robe for the coming child. Soon Zeus began to suffer from pounding headaches and cried out in agony. All the gods came running to help him, and skilled Hephaestus grasped his tools and split open his father's skull. Out sprang Athena, wearing the robe and the helmet, her gray eyes flashing. Thunder roared and the gods stood in awe.

34

Athena's constant companion was Nike, the spirit of victory. With Nike at her side, Athena led armies, but only those that fought for just causes. In time of peace she stood behind the artists of Greece and taught them the fine and useful arts. She had great pride in her own skills at the loom and the potter's wheel, but was happy to see her pupils excel as long as they showed her proper respect.

One of her pupils was Arachne, a simple country girl, who was wonderfully skilled at the loom. People came from far and wide to admire her weavings. Stupidly she boasted that she had learned nothing from Athena; indeed, that she was better than the goddess!

That hurt Athena's pride. Disguised as an old woman, she went to the girl and tried to talk sense into her.

"Your work is beautiful," she said, "but why compare yourself with the gods? Why not be contented to be the best among mortals?"

"Let the goddess Athena herself come and measure her skill against mine," Arachne answered haughtily.

Angrily Athena threw off her disguise and stood before the girl in all her glory.

"Vain girl," she said, "you may have your wish. Sit down at your loom and let us compete."

Athena wove the most beautiful tapestry ever seen, every thread and knot was perfect and the colors sparkled. It pictured the Olympian gods in all their glory and majesty.

Arachne's tapestry was also beautifully woven; Athena herself had to admit that the girl's craftmanship was flawless. But what kind of a picture had she woven? An irreverent scene making fun of Zeus and his wives!

In a wrath the goddess tore the tapestry to shreds and struck the girl with the shuttle. Immediately Arachne felt her head shrink almost to nothing, her nimble fingers change into long, spindly legs. Athena had turned her into a spider.

"Vainglorious girl, go on and spin your thread and weave your empty net forever," said Athena to Arachne, the spider. Athena was a just goddess and she could be very stern. She knew that the gods were great only as long as they were properly worshiped by mortals.

Athena was very fond of a certain city in Greece, and so was her uncle, Poseidon. Both of them claimed the city, and after a long quarrel they decided that the one who could give it the finest gift should have it.

Leading a procession of citizens, the two gods mounted the Acropolis, the flat-topped rock that crowned the city. Poseidon struck the cliff with his trident, and a spring welled up. The people marveled, but the water was salty as the sea that Poseidon ruled, and not very useful. Then Athena gave the city her gift. She planted an olive tree in a crevice on the rock. It was the first olive tree the people had ever seen. Athena's gift was judged the better of the two, for it gave food, oil, and wood, and the city was hers. From her beautiful temple on top of the Acropolis, Athena watched over Athens, her city, with the wise owl, her bird, on her shoulder, and under her leadership the Athenians grew famous for their arts and crafts.

POSEIDON, lord of the sea, was a moody and violent god. His fierce blue eyes pierced the haze, and his sea-blue hair streamed out behind him. He was called the Earthshaker, for when he struck the ground with his trident, the earth trembled and split open. When he struck the sea, waves rose mountain high and the winds howled, wrecking ships and drowning those who lived on the shores. But when he was in a calm mood, he would stretch out his hand and still the sea and raise new lands out of the water.

In the days of Cronus and the Titans, the sea was ruled by Nereus, son of Mother Earth and Pontus, the seas. Nereus was an old sea god with a long gray beard and a fishtail and was the father of fifty sea nymphs, the lovely Nereids. When Poseidon, the Olympian, came to take over the kingdom of the sea, kind old Nereus gave him his daughter Amphitrite for his queen and retired to an underwater grotto. He gave the new king and queen his palace at the bottom of the sea. It was made of the palest gold and lay in a garden of corals and shimmering pearls. There Amphitrite lived contentedly surrounded by her forty-nine Nereid sisters. She had an only son, whose name was Triton. He had a fishtail instead of legs, like his grandfather Nereus, and rode about on the back of a sea monster, trumpeting on a conch shell.

Poseidon was rarely at home. He was a restless god and loved to race the waves with his team of snow-white horses. It was said that he had created the horse in the shape of breaking waves. Like his brother Zeus, Poseidon had many wives and many children, but Amphitrite was not jealous like Hera.

One of the islands that Poseidon raised out of the sea was Delos. It was so newly created that it was still floating about on the water. The little island was barren. Nothing grew on it yet except a single palm tree. In its shade, the two great gods Apollo and Artemis were to be born.

Zeus had married the goddess Leto, and when Hera found out that Leto was expecting twins, she flew into a jealous rage and ordered all the lands in the world to refuse Leto shelter. Chased away from every land, poor Leto wandered from place to place and could not rest to give birth to her twins.

At last she came to Delos and the little island welcomed her. Since it was still floating and not quite land, it was free from Hera's bidding. Exhausted, Leto sank down in the shade of the palm tree, but still she could not give birth to her twins, for Hera forbade Ilithyia, the goddess of childbirth, to go to her. Without her help no child could be born. All the other goddesses felt sorry for Leto and tried to sway Hera by offering her

a beautiful necklace. It was nine yards long, made of gold and amber, and Hera could not resist it. She let Ilithyia go, and Iris whisked her down the rainbow to Leto.

Leto's first child was Artemis, a girl as beautiful as the moon, with hair as dark as the night. She was to be the goddess of the hunt and all newborn creatures. Then Apollo came into the world. He was fair as the sun and he was to be the god of music, light, and reason.

Zeus was filled with joy at the sight of his beautiful twins and he gave them each a silver bow and a quiver full of arrows. The arrows of Artemis were soft as moonbeams and brought painless death, those of Apollo were hard and piercing as the rays of the sun.

Zeus blessed the little island and fastened it to the bottom of the sea. Grass and flowers burst forth from the barren ground, and Delos became the richest of all the Greek islands. Pilgrims flocked to it and loaded it with temples and treasures to honor Leto and her twins.

41

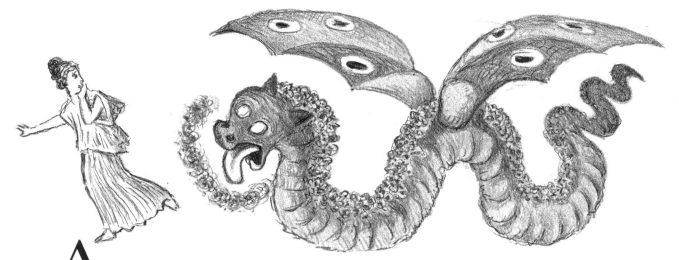

APOLLO grew rapidly, as all gods did, and when he was full grown, Zeus sent him off in a chariot drawn by white swans to win for himself the oracle of Delphi.

No place in Greece was as sacred as Delphi, on the steep slopes of Mount Parnassus. Sulphurous fumes rose from a deep cleft in the mountainside. A sibyl, the priestess of Delphi, sat on a tripod over the cleft and the vapors put her into a magic sleep. In her dreams the sibyl heard the voice of Mother Earth coming up from the depths, and repeated the mystic words she heard. Priests stood around the sibyl and explained the meanings of her muttered prophecies to the pilgrims who had come to the oracle of Delphi to learn about their future.

The oracle was guarded by the darksome dragon Python, who lay coiled around the sacred place. Old age had made him mean and so ill-tempered that the nymphs fled from the sacred spring nearby and the birds no longer dared to sing in the trees.

The oracle had warned Python that Leto's son would one day destroy him. He had tried to devour Leto when she wandered about looking for a place to give birth to her children, but she had escaped. When the old black dragon saw radiant Apollo flying toward him in his golden chariot, he knew that his last hour had come. But he sold his life dearly. He unleashed his fury, spitting fire and venom, and his black scaly body did not stop its writhing and coiling until Apollo had shot him with a thousand of his silver shafts. In torrents did the dragon's venom flow down the mountainside, and the oracle of Delphi was Apollo's.

42   Now there was light and joy on the once-somber slopes of Mount Parnassus. The air was filled with sweet tunes as the birds in the sky and the nymphs of the sacred spring returned to sing Apollo's praise. The voice of the young god rose above all the others, for he was also the god of music.

ARTEMIS, as a newborn goddess, went to her father, Zeus, and asked him to grant her a wish. She wanted to remain forever a wild young maiden hunting through the woods, and she asked him to promise never to make her marry. Zeus consented, and then she asked him for fifty fleet nymphs as companions and a pack of lop-eared hounds to hunt with. Her father gave her all she asked, and she herself caught four hinds with golden antlers and harnessed them to her silver chariot.

When the moon's magic light shone over echoing hills and wooded valleys, Artemis hunted with the nymphs and her hounds. After a wild hunt, the goddess loved to bathe in a quiet pool. Woe to the mortal who happened to see her then!

One night, quite by chance, a young hunter whose name was Actaeon came upon the pool in the woods where Artemis and her nymphs were bathing. He should have taken to his heels and run for his life, but instead, he stood spellbound by the sight of the goddess. Artemis was furious! While the nymphs flung a tunic over her shoulders, the goddess dipped her hand into the pool and threw a handful of water at Actaeon. The moment the silvery drops touched his forehead, antlers sprouted, and rapidly all of Actaeon changed into a stag. His own hounds leaped at him, and, to his horror, he could not utter a human sound to call them off. They brought him down, never knowing that the deer was their own master.

"No mortal shall live to boast that he has seen Artemis bathing," said the goddess, and she picked up her bow and arrows and went on hunting with her nymphs. Artemis was a cold and pitiless goddess.

Apollo and Artemis, though different as day and night, were very fond of each other and they both adored their mother. No one could say a belittling word about gentle Leto without arousing the wrath of her twins.

There was a queen of Thebes whose name was Niobe. She was beautiful and she was rich and she was blessed with fourteen children. Zeus himself was her grandfather, and she was very proud.

"Why worship Leto?" she said to her people. "Build me a temple and worship me in her stead. I have seven sons and seven daughters, while she has only one of each."

When Apollo and Artemis heard this, they grew very angry. Niobe's disrespect could not go unpunished.

Apollo shot his hard arrows at Niobe's seven sons. By no fault of their own, they were torn from life in the prime of their youth. Then Artemis let fly her painless shafts at the seven daughters. Quietly, they lay down on their beds and died.

Niobe's proud heart was broken. She wept for so long that the gods at last took pity on her and changed her into an unfeeling rock. Still, inside the rock, a spring welled up and water like tears trickled down the face of the hard stone.

Apollo had many wives, but Zeus kept his promise to Artemis and never made her marry. Only once she promised her hand to a suitor, but that was a promise she had no intention of keeping. The suitor was Otus, a gigantic son of Poseidon.

Otus and his brother, Ephialtes, were almost sixty feet tall when they reached manhood, and still they went on growing. The gods watched them with concern, for an oracle had predicted that neither gods nor mortals could kill the giant brothers. Mother Earth, however, watched them with pleasure. She was still angry with Zeus for keeping her sons, the Titans, in Tartarus, and she hoped that Otus and Ephialtes would grow big enough to overthrow him.

One night as the brothers slept with their ears to the ground, they heard Mother Earth whisper that such tall and handsome youths should not let themselves be ruled by Zeus. That was just what they had been thinking themselves, for they were vain, as many strong people are. They pulled up mountains, piled them on top of each other, and built a vast new mountain as high as Olympus. From the top they called to Zeus to surrender his powers to them and move out of his palace with the other Olympians. Artemis could stay and become his bride, shouted Otus, and Ephialtes would take Hera.

The two goddesses tossed their heads with scorn, and Zeus in a fury hurled thunderbolts at the ruffians. Zeus's thunderbolts glanced off harmlessly, and when Ares rushed out to fight them, they grabbed him and crammed him into a bronze jar and clamped the lid shut.

For once Zeus was really worried, but Apollo, the god of reason, said that if no one could kill them they must be tricked into killing each other. He persuaded Artemis to pretend that she was in love with Otus. Otus smirked when Apollo called to him that Artemis thought so much of him she had accepted his proposal and would wait for him on the island of Naxos. That made Ephialtes jealous. Why hadn't Hera fallen in love with *him?* Wasn't he as handsome as his brother? But he swallowed his pride and went to Naxos with his brother to meet the bride.

When Artemis saw the two brothers arriving, she quickly changed herself into a white deer and ran across their path. She darted to and fro between them and the brothers, who were eager huntsmen, threw their javelins at the deer. Cleverly, she dodged and the brothers fell to the ground, pierced by each other's javelins. Neither gods nor mortals could kill the giant brothers, but now they had put an end to each other and were thrown into Tartarus, tied back to back with writhing snakes.

All the gods thanked Artemis for saving them, and pulled Ares out of the jar where he had been crouching all the while, howling and screaming.

Orion was another giant son of Poseidon, but, unlike Otus and
Ephialtes, he was modest. He was a great hunter, no beast could escape
from his club and jeweled sword, but he never forgot to praise Artemis as
the greatest of all hunters.

One day Orion, who could walk on water as if it were land, came to
the island of Chios. The island was infested with lions, wolves, and boars
who roared and howled so loudly at night that the King of Chios could
not sleep. He promised Orion the hand of his daughter if he could rid
the island of all the wild beasts. The king's daughter was beautiful, her
father's greatest treasure, and Orion hunted as never before. Soon there
was not a wild beast left, but the king did not want to part with his
daughter, and claimed that he could still hear the howling of wolves at
night. Orion grew angry and threatened to carry off the princess, but the
king soothed him with honeyed words, sent for wine, and filled his cup so
often that Orion drank too much and feel asleep. Stealthily the evil king
crept up and put out both his eyes.

"Now see if you can carry off my daughter," he said.

Blind and helpless, Orion left Chios and staggered over the seas in
search of the sun, which he knew could restore his eyesight, but he could
not find his way. From afar he heard the Cyclopes' hammers and he followed the sound till he came to Hephaestus' forge on the island of Lemnos.
The kind god took pity on him and lent him a Cyclops boy to show him
the way to the East.

With the Cyclops on his shoulders to see for him, Orion walked on

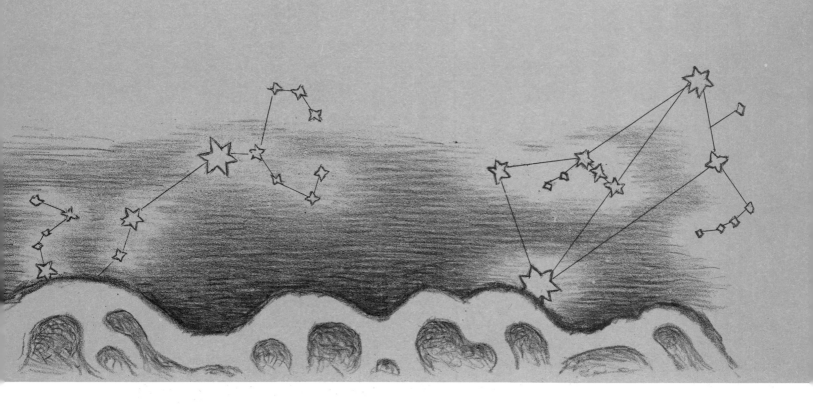

till he met the rising sun. The sun let its healing rays play over Orion's blind eyes, and his sight was restored. Then he rushed back to seek revenge on the false king. But when he arrived, the palace was empty, for the king had seen his huge, menacing shape against the sky and fled with his daughter.

Again Orion went hunting and soon forgot the king and the beautiful princess. He walked from island to island and after a while he came to the island of Crete. There he met the goddess Artemis. She was glad to see him, for he could hunt as well as she and was so very modest about it. Together they hunted wild goats and rejoiced in each other's company. Orion was the only man Artemis had ever favored, and her brother Apollo grew jealous. One day while Artemis was away, he sent an enormous scorpion to attack Orion. Orion's club and mighty sword were no avail against the scorpion's poisonous tail. He turned to flee, but as he did, the giant insect stung his heel.

Artemis was angry with her brother when she returned and found her companion dead. But she could not stay angry with her twin for long, and he helped her hang Orion's image in the skies as a constellation so the great hunter would never be forgotten.

Over the stormy winter sea the constellation of Orion glitters, enormous and menacing, and the dark clouds flee before him like wild animals. But in summer, when the constellation of the Scorpion rises over the horizon, Orion begins to sway and stagger, and then he, in his turn, flees and disappears into the ocean.

HERMES, merriest of the Olympians, was the god of shepherds, travelers, merchants, thieves, and all others who lived by their wits.

His mother Maia, a Titan's daughter, lived in a cave on lofty Mount Cyllene, a cave so deep that Hera never knew that Maia was one of Zeus's wives. Maia had therefore borne her son Hermes in peace.

Hermes was very precocious, even for a god. His mother had hardly wrapped him and put him into a basket when he began to think of mischief. As soon as she had fallen asleep, he wriggled out of his wrappings and tiptoed out of the cave. In the dark of night he toddled straight to the pasture where Apollo kept a large herd of white cows. Apollo liked music better than cows and he did not even notice that Hermes stole into the pasture and picked out the fifty best cows. To keep Apollo from knowing who had stolen his herd and which way they had been driven, Hermes slyly wrapped the hoofs of the cows with bark to disguise their prints, and tied brooms to their tails so they would erase their own tracks. To confuse Apollo even further, he drove the cows backward out of the pasture, and tied bundles of branches to his own little feet so it looked as if a giant had led something into the pasture, but nothing out. He hurried home to

Mount Cyllene and hid the stolen cows in a grove. Two of them he sacrificed to the twelve Olympian gods, not forgetting to include himself as the twelfth! Then he took the entrails of the sacrificed cows, made seven strings of them, and strung them tautly across an empty tortoise shell. When he plucked the strings, they made lovely music. He had invented the first lyre. Pleased with himself, he hid the lyre under his arm and tiptoed back into the cave. He climbed into his basket, closed his eyes, and pretended to be sound asleep, but he did not fool his mother. She knew what he had been up to.

"Shame on you," she said, "sneaking out at night and stealing Apollo's cows."

"Why, Mother!" said Hermes. "I did what I had to do for you and for me. We don't want to live in this dark cave forever. Soon I will be seated on high Olympus as one of the twelve great gods, and you too will live there in glory as my mother." Then he pulled out his lyre and played his mother to sleep with a lullaby.

At dawn Apollo stormed into the cave where Hermes lay in his basket pretending to be asleep. But Apollo wasn't fooled. An oracle had told him who had stolen his herd, and he jerked little Hermes out of his crib and commanded him to return the cows at once.

"How could I have stolen your cows?" Hermes whimpered, "I am only a newborn babe. I don't even know what a cow is. Look for yourself and you can see that there is not a single cow hidden in this cave."

"You are not only a thief but a liar as well," raged Apollo, and chased Hermes out of the cave and straight up to Olympus.

All the gods burst out laughing when they saw innocent-looking little Hermes running with furious Apollo at his heels.

"Tell this thief and liar to give me back my cows at once," said Apollo to their father, Zeus.

"Tell my big brother to stop bullying me. I am a newborn and helpless infant. And I am *not* a liar," said Hermes. "There isn't a cow in my mother's cave."

"If they are not in the cave, then show Apollo where they are," said Zeus, and hid a smile in his beard. He was proud of both his sons and wanted them to be friends.

Hermes had to obey his father, and without any more tricks he led his brother to the woods where the cows were hidden. Apollo forgave him, but when he counted his cows and found that two were missing, his anger flared again. Hermes had expected this and quickly pulled out his lyre and began to play. Apollo listened spellbound to the beautiful sounds from the new musical instrument, and he quite forgot his anger. As the god of music, he must have the lyre and he offered Hermes his whole herd in exchange for the instrument.

Hermes drove a hard bargain and Apollo had to give him his magic wand as well. From then on the two brothers were the best of friends.

Never again did Hermes steal, though he was the god of thieves. He never told a lie, but he didn't always tell the whole truth. His mother, Maia, had no further reasons to be ashamed of him. As the mother of one of the twelve great Olympians, she moved up with him to the glory of Olympus.

Zeus was so delighted with Hermes' ready wit that he made him the herald of the gods. He gave him a golden hat with wings, a pair of winged sandals, and a cape under which he could hide his magic tricks. In a flash

53

he could move from place to place. He put glib words on the tongues of politicians and helped merchants close good bargains. He was as popular among mortals as he was among the gods. Even Hera was fond of him. She had been really angry with him only once, and that was when he had killed her hundred-eyed servant, Argus. Then she was so furious that she demanded he be punished, and called all the great and minor gods to sit in council and judge him. Each god was given a pebble and told to cast his vote according to his decision. Those who found Hermes guilty of a crime were to throw their pebbles at Hera's feet, those who found him innocent were to throw their pebbles at his feet. Hermes talked well in his own defense. Was it a crime to bore someone to death? he asked. After all, that was what he had done to Argus. The gods applauded and so many threw their votes to Hermes that he was completely buried in a heap of pebbles.

Ever after, travelers put up piles of stones along the roads, and they have believed that Hermes stands inside, helping them find their way. These were the first cairns.

Hermes also guided those who set off on their last voyage. He touched the eyes of a dying man with his magic wand and led him down to Hades in the underworld.

HADES, lord of the dead, was a gloomy god of few words. Mortals feared him so much that they did not dare mention his name, for they might attract his attention and he might send for them. Instead of Hades they called him the Rich One, and indeed, rich he was. All the treasures in the ground belonged to him. They also called him the Hospitable One, for in his desolate underground realm he always had room for another dead soul.

Hermes guided the souls of the dead down to the brink of the river Styx, a murky, stagnant river that flowed around the underworld. There Hermes left them in charge of the ferryman Charon. If they had money to pay for their fare, Charon set them across. If not, he refused to take them, for he was greedy. Those who could not pay had to wander about till they found the pauper's entrance to Hades. That is why, when a man died, his kin put a coin under his tongue.

Sooner or later, all mortals came to Hades. Once inside his realm, they whirled about forever like dry leaves in a cold autumn wind. Cerberus, the three-headed watchdog of the underworld, stood at the gates. He let the dead souls enter, but, once past his gnashing teeth and spiked tail, they could never go out again.

Hades lived in a dark and gloomy palace with his ice-cold queen, Persephone. She was beautiful, but as silent and somber as her husband, for she wasn't happy. She had not come to rule the joyless underworld of her own free will. She had been kidnaped by Hades.

PERSEPHONE grew up on Olympus and her gay laughter rang through the brilliant halls. She was the daughter of Demeter, goddess of the harvest, and her mother loved her so dearly she could not bear to have her out of her sight. When Demeter sat on her golden throne, her daughter was always on her lap; when she went down to earth to look after her trees and fields, she took Persephone. Wherever Persephone danced on her light feet, flowers sprang up. She was so lovely and full of grace that even Hades, who saw so little, noticed her and fell in love with her. He wanted her for his queen, but he knew that her mother would never consent to part with her, so he decided to carry her off.

One day as Persephone ran about in the meadow gathering flowers, she strayed away from her mother and the attending nymphs. Suddenly, the ground split open and up from the yawning crevice came a dark chariot drawn by black horses. At the reins stood grim Hades. He seized the terrified girl, turned his horses, and plunged back into the ground. A herd of pigs rooting in the meadow tumbled into the cleft, and Persephone's cries for help died out as the ground closed again as suddenly as it had opened. Up in the field, a little swineherd stood and wept over the pigs he had lost, while Demeter rushed wildly about in the meadow, looking in vain for her daughter, who had vanished without leaving a trace.

With the frightened girl in his arms, Hades raced his snorting horses down away from the sunlit world. Down and down they sped on the dark path to his dismal underground palace. He led weeping Persephone in,

seated her beside him on a throne of black marble, and decked her with gold and precious stones. But the jewels brought her no joy. She wanted no cold stones. She longed for warm sunshine and flowers and her golden-tressed mother.

Dead souls crowded out from cracks and crevices to look at their new queen, while ever more souls came across the Styx and Persephone watched them drink from a spring under dark poplars. It was the spring of Lethe, and those who drank from its waters forgot who they were and what they had done on earth. Rhadamanthus, a judge of the dead, dealt out punishment to the souls of great sinners. They were sentenced to suffer forever under the whips of the avenging Erinyes. Heroes were led to the Elysian fields, where they lived happily forever in never-failing light.

Around the palace of Hades there was a garden where whispering poplars and weeping willows grew. They had no flowers and bore no fruit and no birds sang in their branches. There was only one tree in the whole realm of Hades that bore fruit. That was a little pomegranate tree. The gardener of the underworld offered the tempting pomegranates to the queen, but Persephone refused to touch the food of the dead.

Wordlessly she walked through the garden at silent Hades' side and slowly her heart turned to ice.

Above, on earth, Demeter ran about searching for her lost daughter, and all nature grieved with her. Flowers wilted, trees lost their leaves, and the fields grew barren and cold. In vain did the plow cut through the icy ground; nothing could sprout and nothing could grow while the goddess of the harvest wept. People and animals starved and the gods begged Demeter again to bless the earth. But she refused to let anything grow until she had found her daughter.

Bent with grief, Demeter turned into a gray old woman. She returned to the meadow where Persephone had vanished and asked the sun if he had seen what had happened, but he said no, dark clouds had hidden his face that day. She wandered around the meadow and after a while she met a youth whose name was Triptolemus. He told her that his brother, a swineherd, had seen his pigs disappear into the ground and had heard the frightened screams of a girl.

Demeter now understood that Hades had kidnaped her daughter, and her grief turned to anger. She called to Zeus and said that she would never again make the earth green if he did not command Hades to return

Persephone. Zeus could not let the world perish and he sent Hermes down to Hades, bidding him to let Persephone go. Even Hades had to obey the orders of Zeus, and sadly he said farewell to his queen.

Joyfully, Persephone leaped to her feet, but as she was leaving with Hermes, a hooting laugh came from the garden. There stood the gardener of Hades, grinning. He pointed to a pomegranate from which a few of the kernels were missing. Persephone, lost in thought, had eaten the seeds, he said.

Then dark Hades smiled. He watched Hermes lead Persephone up to the bright world above. He knew that she must return to him, for she had tasted the food of the dead.

When Persephone again appeared on earth, Demeter sprang to her feet with a cry of joy and rushed to greet her daughter. No longer was she a sad old woman, but a radiant goddess. Again she blessed her fields and the flowers bloomed anew and the grain ripened.

"Dear child," she said, "never again shall we be parted. Together we shall make all nature bloom." But joy soon was changed to sadness, for Persephone had to admit that she had tasted the food of the dead and must return to Hades. However, Zeus decided that mother and daughter should not be parted forever. He ruled that Persephone had to return to Hades and spend one month in the underworld for each seed she had eaten.

Every year, when Persephone left her, Demeter grieved, nothing grew, and there was winter on earth. But as soon as her daughter's light footsteps were heard, the whole earth burst into bloom. Spring had come. As long as mother and daughter were together, the earth was warm and bore fruit.

Demeter was a kind goddess. She did not want mankind to starve during the cold months of winter when Persephone was away. She lent her chariot, laden with grain, to Triptolemus, the youth who had helped her to find her lost daughter. She told him to scatter her golden grain over the world and teach men how to sow it in spring and reap it in fall and store it away for the long months when again the earth was barren and cold.

DIONYSUS, the god of wine, was the youngest of the Olympians. He was the only one of the twelve great gods whose mother was a mortal. His father was Zeus himself.

Jealous Hera hated his mother, the beautiful princess Semele, and one day when Zeus was away, the goddess disguised herself as an old crone and went to visit her. She talked about this and about that, pretending to be very friendly, and then she asked why Semele's husband was not at home, and what kind of man he might be.

"He is nobody less than mighty Zeus," Semele said proudly.

"How can you be so sure about that?" said the old woman. "I know many husbands who claim to be the lord of all creation. Do you have proof that he really is who he says he is? If I were you, I would ask him to show himself in all his splendor." Then she went away, and Semele was left alone, wondering.

When Zeus returned, Semele asked him to grant her a wish. Zeus, who loved her dearly, swore by the river Styx to fulfill any wish she might have.

"Then show yourself in all your splendor," said Semele. Zeus begged her to change her wish, for he knew that no mortal eyes could bear the sight of him when he revealed himself as the flashing thunder-god, a hundred times brighter than the sun. But Hera had planted the seed of suspicion so deep in Semele's heart that she refused to change her wish. Zeus had to keep his promise, for he had sworn by the river Styx, the most solemn oath of the gods.

He joined together the smallest storm clouds he could find, chose his tiniest lightning bolt, and showed himself to Semele as the mighty thunder-god. Even so, he was so brilliant that Semele caught fire and burned to cinders. Zeus could do nothing to save her. She went down to Hades as a fluttering ghost. Zeus barely managed to rescue her unborn son, and sewed him under the skin of his own leg, and when the child was ready to be born, he sprang forth as the immortal god Dionysus.

Zeus knew well enough who was the cause of Semele's death, and he gave her little son to Hermes and told him to hide the boy from Hera. Hermes carried Dionysus to the faraway valley of Nysa, and left him in the care of a band of Maenads, the nymphs of the valley. There Dionysus grew up with tigers and leopards for playmates.

Large bunches of purple grapes grew on the sunny slope of the valley of Nysa, and in time Dionysus invented the making of wine from their juice. As a young and beautiful god, dressed in flowing robes of royal purple, he went out into the world to teach men how to make wine. The Maenads went with him, and so did the leopards and tigers, and ever more followers joined him. Wherever he went he was worshiped as a new god, and his father, Zeus, watched him with pleasure.

Dionysus returned to Greece and traveled from island to island teaching the making of wine. One day as he was sleeping alone on a beach, a pirate ship sailed by. When the pirates saw the richly clad youth, they thought he was a prince and carried him off on their ship to hold him for ransom. He did not wake from his heavy slumber till the ship was far out at sea. With gentle words he tried to persuade the pirates to take him back; he was not a prince, he said, he was the god of wine, and his riches were not of this world. The pirates laughed scornfully and sailed on, paying him no heed.

Suddenly their laughter died, for out of the sea sprouted vines loaded with grapes. They grew, twining around the oars, winding up the mast, and spreading over the whole ship as though it were an arbor. Blood-red wine dripped down the sail and the air was filled with the sound of roaring tigers and braying asses. Dionysus himself seemed to grow till he filled the ship with his glory. Horrified, the sailors threw themselves into the sea, but they did not drown, for Dionysus was a kind god. He changed them into dolphins, and that is why dolphins are the most human of all creatures that live in the ocean.

66

Dionysus had brought much joy to mankind, and Zeus decided that
the time had come to give him a golden throne on Olympus. Hera rose
in anger and said she refused to share the hall with the son of a mortal
woman, but Zeus pounded his indomitable fist and Hera sat silent.

68   There were only twelve thrones in the hall, so kind Hestia quietly
rose from hers and said that Dionysus could have it. Her place was at
the hearth, she said; she needed no throne.

Before seating himself on his throne Dionysus asked to see his mother

for whom he had always longed. Zeus not only permitted him to see her, but let him go down to Hades and bring her up to the glory of Olympus, for she was now the mother of one of the great gods. Happily Dionysus entered the hall and seated himself on his golden throne. The air was filled with the music of flutes and tambourines. Never had there been such a din and merriment on Olympus. Zeus looked around with great content and beckoned to his cupbearer, Ganymede, bidding him fill the golden goblets with sweet nectar.

69

MINOR GODS,
NYMPHS, SATYRS AND CENTAURS

MINOR GODS AND GODDESSES also lived on Olympus besides the twelve great ones. The most powerful of them were the goddesses of destiny, Clotho, Lachesis, and Atropos. They were the three Fates and they decided how long a mortal would live and how long the rule of the gods should last. When a mortal was born, Clotho spun the thread of life, Lachesis measured a certain length, and Atropos cut the thread at the end of the life. They knew the past and the future, and even Zeus had no power to sway their decisions. Their sister, Nemesis, saw to it that all evil and all good on earth were justly repaid, and all mortals feared her.

Man's creator and his best friend was the Titan Prometheus. Zeus had given Prometheus and his brother, Epimetheus, the task of repopu-

lating the earth after all living creatures had perished in the early battles of the gods. He gave the two brothers great measures of gifts to bestow upon their creations, and they went down to earth and began to make men and beasts out of river clay. Wise Prometheus modeled men with great care in the shape of the gods. Epimetheus rapidly made all kinds of animals and without any foresight he lavished the good gifts upon them. When Prometheus had finished shaping man, he found that there were few of the good gifts left. Animals could run faster, see, smell, and hear better, and had much more endurance. Besides, they were kept snug in their warm coats of fur, while men shivered in the cold nights.

Prometheus was sorry for mankind and he went to Zeus and asked him if he might have some of the sacred fire for his poor creations. But Zeus said no, fire belonged to the gods alone.

71

Prometheus could not bear to see his people suffer and he decided to steal fire, though he knew that Zeus would punish him severely. He went up to Olympus, took a glowing ember from the sacred hearth, and hid it in a hollow stalk of fennel. He carried it down to earth, gave it to mankind, and told them never to let the light from Olympus die out. No longer did men shiver in the cold of the night, and the beasts feared the light of the fire and did not dare to attack them.

A strange thing happened: as men lifted their eyes from the ground and watched the smoke from their fires spiraling upward, their thoughts rose with it up to the heavens. They began to wonder and think, and were no longer earth-bound clods. They built temples to honor the gods and, wanting to share what they had with them, they burned the best pieces of meat on their altars.

Zeus was furious when he first saw the fires flickering on earth, but he was appeased when the savory scent of roast meat reached his nostrils. All the gods loved the smell of the burnt offerings; it spiced their daily food of ambrosia and nectar. But Prometheus knew how hard men worked to make their living and thought it a pity that they burned up the best parts of their food. He told them to butcher an ox and divide the meat in two equal heaps. In one were the chops and roasts, hidden under sinews and bones. In the other were scraps and entrails, covered with snow-white fat. Prometheus then invited Zeus to come down to earth and choose for himself which part he wanted for his burnt offerings. Zeus, of course, chose the best-looking heap, but when he discovered that he had been tricked he grew very angry. Not only had Prometheus stolen the sacred fire and given it to men, he had also taught them to cheat the gods. He resolved to punish both Prometheus and his creations.

Cast in unbreakable irons, Prometheus was chained to the top of the Caucasus Mountains. Every day an eagle swooped out of the sky and ate his liver. At night his immortal liver grew anew, but every day the eagle returned and he had to suffer again.

72

Thus was Prometheus punished. But Zeus found a more subtle way to punish the mortals. He sent to earth a beautiful but silly woman. Her name was Pandora.

PANDORA was modeled by Hephaestus in the likeness of Aphrodite. He carved her out of a block of white marble, made her lips of red rubies and her eyes of sparkling sapphires. Athena breathed life into her and dressed her in elegant garments. Aphrodite decked her with jewels and fixed her red mouth in a winning smile. Into the mind of this beautiful creature, Zeus put insatiable curiosity, and then he gave her a sealed jar and warned her never to open it.

Hermes brought Pandora down to earth and offered her in marriage to Epimetheus, who lived among the mortals. Epimetheus had been warned by Prometheus never to accept a gift from Zeus, but he could not resist the beautiful woman. Thus Pandora came to live among mortals, and men came from near and far to stand awestruck by her wondrous beauty.

But Pandora was not perfectly happy, for she did not know what was in the jar that Zeus had given her. It was not long before her curiosity got the better of her and she had to take a quick peek.

The moment she opened the lid, out swarmed a horde of miseries: Greed, Vanity, Slander, Envy, and all the evils that until then had been unknown to mankind. Horrified at what she had done, Pandora clapped the lid on, just in time to keep Hope from flying away too. Zeus had put Hope at the bottom of the jar, and the unleashed miseries would quickly have put an end to it. They stung and bit the mortals as Zeus had planned, but their sufferings made them wicked instead of good, as Zeus had hoped. They lied, they stole, and they killed each other and became so evil that Zeus in disgust decided to drown them in a flood.

But there was one man on earth who had not turned evil. He was a son of Prometheus. His name was Deucalion.

DEUCALION often went to the Caucasus Mountains to comfort his suffering father. He could not break the chains that bound him, but while he was there, he could keep away the eagle that tortured Prometheus. Deucalion was a good son, and his father was thankful for his help.

Prometheus, who could look into the future, knew that Zeus was planning to flood the earth. He told his son to build an ark and board it with Pyrrha, his virtuous wife.

Deucalion did as his father told him. He built a sturdy ark, and when Zeus let loose all the winds and opened wide the floodgates of the sky, he went aboard with Pyrrha. For nine days and nine nights it rained until the whole earth was flooded. Nothing but the highest mountain peaks remained above water and all mortals were drowned. Only Deucalion and Pyrrha were saved; they floated in their ark over the deep, dark waters.

On the tenth day, the rain stopped, and slowly dry land began to appear. Deucalion and Pyrrha stepped out of the ark and walked about

on the desolate earth. Lonesome and forlorn, they came to a temple, grown over with seaweed, and entered it. The sacred fire on the altar had gone out, but they lit it again with the embers they had kept glowing aboard the ark, and lifted up their hands in prayer to the gods to thank them for saving their lives. Zeus was touched by their piety and felt sorry for them because they were so lonesome. He spoke to them and said: "Pick up the bones of your mother and throw them over your shoulders."

Deucalion understood that Zeus did not mean their mortal mothers, but their Mother Earth. Rocks were her bones. He told Pyrrha to pick up a handful of stones and throw them over her shoulder while he did the same. Behind Deucalion, a score of men sprang up, and there, behind Pyrrha, a score of women. This new race of mortals was called Deucalion's race.

The Deucalion race, made from stone, was hardier than the one made from clay. The new mortals withstood better the stings of Pandora's miseries, which of course, had flown high and dry during the flood, and plague mankind to this very day.

77

The winds had carried on as they wished when Zeus flooded the earth. They were powerful fellows, and when they stormed together, they brought confusion and destruction, whirling dust and water all the way up to Olympus. Zeus decided that they needed a dependable guardian who would keep them locked up and let out only one at a time. He chose Aeolus, a grandson of Deucalion and Pyrrha, to be the keeper of the winds and sent him to live with them and guard them in a hollow cliff, far out at sea.

The winds hated to be confined. They stormed and howled around Aeolus, trying to force their way out of the cavern, but Aeolus was steady and strong and kept them in hand. When Poseidon or one of the other gods called for a wind, Aeolus pierced the wall of the cliff with his spear

and let the wind out. Then he plugged up the hole and kept it closed until it was time for the wind to return.

When Boreas, the North Wind, was called for, he rushed out, icy and wild, tearing up trees and piling up waves in front of him.

When Notus, the South Wind, was let out, he pressed himself groaning through the hole in the cliff. He was so heavy with moisture that water dripped from his tangled beard, and he spread a leaden fog over land and sea. Wanderers lost their paths and ships drifted helplessly about.

Zephyr, the West Wind, was gentler than his brothers. When he blew, he swept the sky clear of clouds and all nature smiled.

Eurus, the East Wind, was the least important of the brothers. He wasn't called for often.

79

EOS, gentle dawn, was the mother of the four winds. While all creation slept, she rose from her pink pillows to announce the coming of a new day. She dipped her rosy fingers into a cup filled with dew and sprinkled the drops over flowers and trees. All nature awoke, rejoicing to see her.

One morning as Eos looked down on earth, her eyes fell on a young prince waking from his slumber. He was so handsome she could not take her eyes off him, and she wanted him for her husband. But how could she, who was a goddess, be married to a mortal whose life span was so short?

As soon as her morning duties were done, she went to Zeus and persuaded him to grant eternal life to the young prince, whose name was Tithonus.

She brought him with her to her palace in the east, and they spent many delightful years together.

But Eos had forgotten to ask that Tithonus be also given eternal youth, and slowly his strength left his once-supple limbs. He shriveled and shrank, and his manly voice changed to a feeble squeak. He shrank to a tiny, wizened old man, yet he could not die, for he had been given eternal life. He became so small and weak that Eos had to put him into a little basket and hide him in a corner of her palace. There, in his dark corner, he went on withering and shriveling till at last he turned into a grasshopper, chirping for all eternity.

But Eos stayed rosy and young, always a joy to behold when she came out to wake the sleeping world and announce the coming of her brother, the sun.

Helios, the sun, mounted his glowing chariot and drove out in great splendor as soon as Eos threw open the gates of his golden palace in the east. His radiance lit up the wide expanse of sky. So bright was he that only the gods could look straight at him without being blinded. Brilliant rays encircled his head, and his chariot glowed like fire.

With a strong hand, Helios guided his four fiery steeds up the vault of the heavens. The path was steep and narrow and the horses were wild, but Helios held them well on their course. At high noon, he stopped at the top of the sky and looked around, and nothing could escape his piercing gaze. Again he drove on and now he gave free rein to his steeds. Far to the west they could see his glittering evening palace, and, eager to reach their stables, they raced on the downhill course, faster and faster. They passed a great herd of white cows hurrying homeward to Helios' palace and met a large flock of sheep going out to pasture in the sky. For Helios owned a snow-white cow for each day of the year and a woolly sheep for each night.

The shadows grew long and dusk settled over the world when Helios and his foaming team arrived. His five daughters, the Heliades, awaited them. They unharnessed the tired horses and let them plunge into the ocean for a cooling bath. Then the horses rested in their stables and Helios talked with his daughters and told them all he had seen that day.

In the dark of the night, he boarded a vessel of gold with his team and sailed around the world, back to his palace in the east. The way was far shorter by sea than by air, so he had time to stay for a while in his morning palace too before he set out on another day's journey.

Helios had a son named Phaëthon. He was a mortal and very proud of his radiant father. One morning as Helios was about to set off on his daily journey across the sky, Phaëthon came to him and begged him to grant his dearest wish. Helios, who was very fond of his handsome son, rashly swore by the river Styx to give him any wish he might have, but when he heard Phaëthon's wish, he sorely regretted his oath. He tried in vain to make his son change his mind, for what Phaëthon wanted was to drive the sun chariot for one day, and Helios knew that no one but he himself could handle the spirited steeds.

Phaëthon was determined to have his wish, and Helios had to give in. Sadly, he put his golden rays on his son's head and rubbed divine

82

ointment on his skin so he could withstand the searing heat of the chariot. He barely had time to warn him to stay well in the middle of the heavenly path when the gates of the palace were thrown open, and the rearing horses were brought forth. Phaëthon leaped into the chariot, grasped the reins, and the horses rushed out.

At first, all went well and Phaëthon stood proudly in the glowing chariot. But the fiery steeds soon felt that unskilled hands were holding the reins. They veered off the heavenly path and brushed by the dangerous constellations that lurked on both sides of it. The animals of the zodiac were enraged: the bull charged, the lion growled, the scorpion lashed out with its poisonous tail. The horses shied and Phaëthon was thrown halfway out of the chariot. Far down below he saw the earth and he grew so dizzy that he dropped the reins. Without a firm hand to guide them, the horses bolted. They raced so close to the earth that the ground cracked from the heat of the chariot and rivers and lakes dried up. Then upward they sped so high that the earth froze and turned to ice.

Zeus stood on Olympus and shook his head. He had to stop the careening chariot to save the earth from destruction, and he threw a thunderbolt at it. In a shower of sparks, the chariot flew apart and Phaëthon plunged into the river Po. On the riverbanks his sisters mourned so long that Zeus took pity on them and changed them into poplar trees and their tears into drops of golden amber.

Hephaestus had to work the whole night through to mend the broken chariot so Helios could drive it again the next day. Helios grieved over his lost son, and he never again allowed anyone to drive his chariot except for Apollo, the god of light.

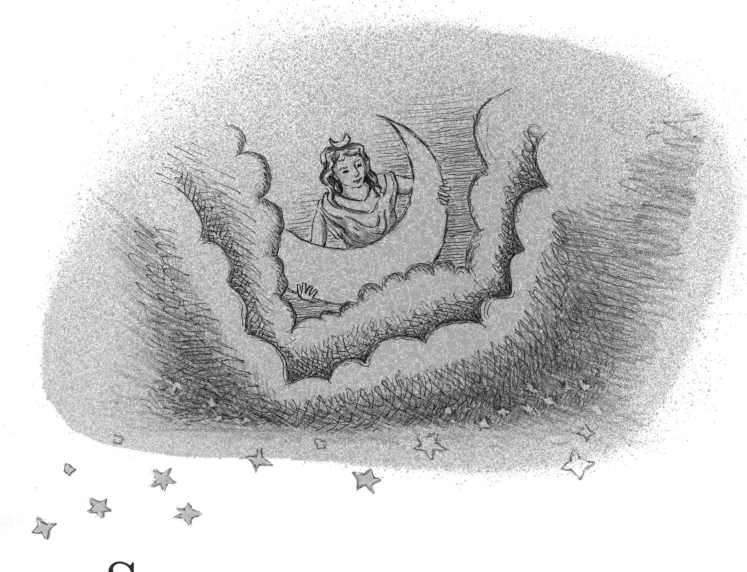

SELENE, the moon, came out at night to light up the world while her brother, Helios, was resting. Slowly she drove her milk-white horses across the sky, and her pale moonbeams fell gently on the sleeping earth where all was peace and quiet.

One night Selene's soft light fell on Endymion, a young shepherd, who was sleeping beside his flock. She stopped to look at him. He was smiling in his sleep and was so young and handsome that she completely lost her heart to him. She drove through the night, but she could not get him out of her mind.

When her duties were over, she went to Zeus and asked him to grant Endymion eternal sleep so he would stay forever young and handsome. She had learned from her sister, Eos, not to ask for eternal life for a mortal and be left with a grasshopper on her hands.

Zeus granted Selene's wish and Endymion slept on and on, smiling in his sleep. He dreamed that he held the moon in his arms. But it was not a dream after all, for Selene bore her husband fifty daughters, all pale and beautiful as their mother and sleepy as their father.

In Selene's magic light, river-gods rose from silvery streams to inspect
their river beds, and hills trembled under the hoofs of the wild centaurs.

Laughing nymphs and bleating satyrs danced to the music of Pan, god of
nature, master of them all.

PAN, the great god of nature, was not a handsome god. He had goat's legs, pointed ears, a pair of small horns, and he was covered all over with dark, shaggy hair. He was so ugly that his mother, a nymph, ran away screaming when she first saw him. But his father, Hermes, was delighted with the strange looks of his son. He carried him up to Olympus to amuse the other gods and they all laughed and took him to their hearts. They called him Pan and sent him back to the dark woods and stony hills of Greece as the great god of nature. He was to be the protector of hunters, shepherds, and curly-fleeced sheep.

Pan was a lonely and moody god. When he was sad, he went off by himself and hid in a cool cave. If a wanderer happened to come upon him and disturb him in his retreat, he would let out a scream so bone-chilling that whoever heard it took to his heels and fled in a fear that they called panic.

But when Pan was in a good mood, and that was mostly on moon-lit nights, he cavorted through glades and forests, and up steep mountain slopes playing on his shepherd's pipe, and nymphs and satyrs followed dancing behind him. Sweet and unearthly were the tunes that floated over the hills.

The satyrs much resembled their master, Pan, but they were mischievous and good for nothing except for chasing nymphs. Old satyrs, or sileni, were fat and too lazy to walk. They rode about on asses, but they often fell off, since they were fond of drinking wine.

The lightfooted nymphs always looked young, though some of them were very old in years. Their life span was so long that they were almost immortal: they lived ten thousand times longer than man. There were water nymphs and nymphs of mountains and glens. There were nymphs who lived in trees and nymphs who lived in springs.

When a tree grew old and rotted, the nymph who lived in it moved to another tree of the same kind. A wood chopper, about to fell a healthy tree, must remember first to ask permission of the tree nymph. If he did not, she might send out a swarm of bees to sting him, or she might turn the ax in his hands so he would cut his own leg instead of the tree trunk.

A thirsty hunter must never drink from a spring without asking the water nymph's permission. If he ignored the nymph, she might send a venomous water snake to bite him, or she might poison the water and make him sick.

River-gods, too, had to be asked before anyone took water from their rivers. They were usually helpful and friendly to men and willingly shared their water, but woe to the one who tried to carry off their water-nymph daughters. They would rush out of their river beds and charge him in full river-god rage. They were dangerous opponents, for they grew oxhorns on their heads and could change their shapes at will. Zeus himself feared their rage, and Pan and the satyrs kept well out of their way, though Pan liked all nymphs and fell in love with many of them.

ECHO was one of the nymphs with whom Pan fell in love. She was a gay nymph who chattered and prattled all day long and never kept quiet long enough for Pan to win her with music and poetry.

One day Hera came down from Olympus to look for Zeus. She suspected that he was playing with the nymphs, but Echo detained her so long with idle chatter that Zeus, who really was there, was able to sneak away. Hera, in a rage, punished Echo by taking from her the gift of forming her own words. From then on poor Echo could only repeat the words of others.

Now at last Pan thought he could win her by his words. But before he had a chance, she had lost her heart to another. He was Narcissus, and he was so handsome that every girl and every nymph he met fell in love with him. Unfortunately, he liked nobody but himself.

Echo trailed silently behind Narcissus as he hunted in the woods, hoping to hear an endearing word from him that she could repeat. But he never so much as noticed her. At last toward nightfall, they came to a quiet pool, and as Narcissus was thirsty, he bent down to drink. Suddenly, he stopped and stared, for in the mirroring surface of the water he saw the handsomest face he had ever seen. He smiled and the handsome face smiled back at him. Joyfully he nodded and so did the stranger in the water.

"I love you," said Narcissus to the handsome face.

"I love you," repeated Echo eagerly. She stood behind him, happy to be able to speak to him at last.

But Narcissus neither saw nor heard her; he was spellbound by the handsome stranger in the water. He did not know that it was his own image that he had fallen in love with and he sat smiling at himself, forgetting to eat, forgetting to drink, until he wasted away and died. Hermes came and led him down to the realm of the dead, but where he had been sitting the lovely Narcissus flower sprang up. Echo stood beside the flower and grieved and pined until she too faded away.

Nothing was left of Echo but her voice, which to this day can be heard senselessly repeating the words of others.

Pan grieved for a while, but then another pretty nymph crossed his path and he forgot all about Echo. Her name was Syrinx.

Syrinx ran away from Pan; she thought he was so ugly. Pan chased after her, and, to escape from him, she changed herself into a reed. She stood among hundreds of other reeds on the riverbank, and Pan couldn't find her. As he walked through the reed patch, sighing and looking for her in vain, the wind blew through the reeds. They swayed and bent and made a plaintive whistling sound. Pan listened, enchanted. "Thus you and I shall always sing together," he said.

He cut ten reeds into unequal lengths, tied them together, and made the first panpipe. He called the new instrument his syrinx, for every time he played on it he thought he heard the melodious voice of his beloved nymph. Again Pan was lonesome and he retreated to his cool cave, deep in the woods, and scared away all passers-by with his unearthly screams.

Splendid Apollo himself fared no better than Pan when he fell in love with a nymph called Daphne. Daphne had a cold heart, she had vowed never to marry, and when Apollo wooed her, she would not listen to the sound of his golden lyre and ran away. As she fled, she was lovelier still, with her golden hair streaming behind her, and Apollo could not bear to lose her. He set off in pursuit, beseeching her to stop. Daphne ran to-

ward the bank of a river that belonged to her father, the river-god Ladon, calling to him to save her from her pursuer. Ladon had no time to rise out of his river bed and come to his daughter's rescue, but the moment Daphne's toes touched the sand of the riverbank, he changed them into roots. Apollo, who was close at her heels, caught up with her, but the instant he threw his arms about her, her arms changed into branches, her lovely head into the crown of a tree, and she became a laurel. Still, inside the hard bark, Apollo could hear the beating of Daphne's frightened heart.

Apollo carefully broke off some twigs and made a wreath of the shining leaves.

"Fair nymph," he said, "you would not be my bride, but at least consent to be my tree and your leaves shall crown my brow."

Ever after, the greatest honor an artist or a hero could be given was to be crowned with a wreath from Apollo's sacred tree, the laurel.

Daphne would rather be an unmoving tree than the bride of the great god Apollo, but all the other nymphs loved to sit at his feet and listen to his enchanting music, and were very honored when he or any of the other great Olympian gods chose one of them as a bride.

95

THE WILD AND VULGAR CENTAURS did not honor any of the gods. They were half men and half horses, as cunning as wild men and as savage as untamed horses. They had inherited the worst dispositions of both.

The first centaurs had come tumbling out of a cloud that their father, Ixion, King of the Lapith people, had married, mistaking it for the goddess Hera. Zeus had created the cloud to test the ungodliness of the wicked king who wanted to carry off Hera. Ixion was severely punished for his ungodliness. He was condemned to whirl about forever in the underworld, tied to a flaming wheel, but his offspring, the centaurs, remained on earth as a scourge to the Lapith people.

The centaurs lived without law and order, stormed over fields, trampled crops, and carried off the Lapith women, and they ate raw meat. The young centaurs were no better than their elders. They were poorly brought up by parents who kicked them and spanked them and left them to fend for themselves.

There was one centaur who was kind and wise and was fond of children. His name was Chiron. Though he looked like the other centaurs, he wasn't related to them at all. He was the son of Cronus the Titan and was immortal. Chiron was famous as the greatest teacher in Greece. Kings brought their small sons to him so he could raise them in the true spirit of heroes.

In his quiet cave on Mount Pelion, he taught them manly sports and how to use the healing herbs of the earth and how to read the stars in the sky. All his pupils returned to their homes exceeding their fathers in courage and knowledge.

One day Apollo brought to Chiron his little mortal son, Asclepius. His mother, a Lapith princess, had died, and Apollo asked Chiron to raise the boy.

ASCLEPIUS grew up in Chiron's cave, raised with loving care, and, being the son of Apollo, he soon surpassed his foster father in his knowledge of healing the sick.

When he was grown, he left Chiron's cave and went down from the mountain to help the people of Greece. He became the first great physician. People flocked to him from far and near, and many who came on crutches went away skipping and dancing. His patients adored him and showered treasures upon him, and it wasn't long before they worshiped him as a god and built temples in his honor. Asclepius put beds in his temples and they became the first hospitals. There he went about from bed to bed, pleased to be looked upon as a god, leaning on a staff entwined with sacred serpents. Serpents knew all the secrets of the earth and often told him the causes and cures for diseases. Sometimes he put his patients to sleep with a magic draught and listened to what they muttered in their dreams. Their words often revealed to him what caused their ailments, and he could then find a cure for them.

Asclepius had a wife and seven children, and all the children followed in their father's footsteps. His sons were his assistant physicians, his daughters were his nurses. Hygeia, one of his daughters, washed and scrubbed her patients from morning to night, and it was a marvel to see how fast they regained their health. Before Hygeia's time, it was thought that soap and water would kill the sick.

Asclepius grew famous, rich, and pink-faced, and as time went on, he grew so skilled in his art that he could even bring the dead back to life. The Fates became upset and complained to Zeus that they measured and clipped the threads of life in vain. Hades too was angry, for he was being cheated out of dead souls. Apollo pointed out to Zeus how much good his son was doing for mankind, and for a while Zeus was lenient. But when Asclepius accepted gold for bringing the dead back to life, Zeus hurled a thunderbolt at him.

Nothing but a small heap of ashes was left of Asclepius, the first great doctor. But his temples and his teachings of medical science remained, and the gods put his image among the stars as a constellation.

Apollo was furious with Zeus for killing his son and wanted revenge. He did not dare to raise his hand against his mighty father, but he slew the Cyclopes who had given Zeus the thunderbolt. Zeus, in his turn, had to revenge the Cyclopes. He punished Apollo by making him serve for a year as a slave on earth.

Apollo found a good master and suffered no hardship. But the gods on high Olympus missed him and his music, the nine Muses most of all.

ERATO
Muse of Lyrics

EUTERPE
Muse of Music

THALIA
Muse of Comedy

MELPOMENE
Muse of Tragedy

TERPSICHORE
Muse of Dance

THE NINE MUSES were daughters of Zeus and the Titaness Mnemosyne. Their mother's memory was as long as her beautiful hair, for she was the goddess of memory and knew all that had happened since the beginning of time. She gathered her nine daughters around her and told them wondrous tales. She told them about the creation of earth and the fall of the Titans, about the glorious Olympians and their rise to power, about Prometheus, who stole the heavenly fire, about the sun and the stars, and most of all about the greatness and wisdom of their father, Zeus. The nine Muses listened to her with wide, sparkling eyes and turned her stories into poems and songs so they would never be forgotten.

Apollo, the god of music, trained them and taught them to sing

URANIA
Muse of Astronomy

CLIO
Muse of History

POLYHYMNIA
Muse of Hymns

ORPHEUS

CALLIOPE
Muse of Epics

harmoniously together. He led the choir of Muses through the halls of Olympus and over the slopes of Mount Parnassus, and their music rang so pure and fine that even the songbirds fell silent to listen.

Each of the Muses had her own special art. Calliope, the Muse of heroic poetry, was the first among them. She had a mortal son named Orpheus, and he sang almost as beautifully as the Muses themselves. When he was grown, he left his mother and his eight loving aunts and went to live in his father's kingdom of Thrace to bring the joy of music to earth. His voice rang so pure and true that the fiercest warriors put down their swords and savage beasts lay spellbound at his feet. Trees pulled up their roots and moved closer to listen, and even hard rocks rolled up to him.

ORPHEUS' music was joyful and gay, for he was in love with Euridice, a sweet young maiden, and she loved him in return. On the day of their wedding, his songs swelled out, filled with happiness as his bride danced on light feet through the meadow. Suddenly, she trod on a snake and sank to the ground, dead of its poisonous bite. Hermes gently closed her eyes and led her away to the underworld. No more songs came from Orpheus' throat, no more tunes rang out from his lyre. All joy had gone out of his life. He had to have his Euridice back.

Weeping and grieving, Orpheus wandered about searching for an entrance to Hades, and when at the end of the world he found it, he did what no living man had ever done before: he went down to the realm of the dead to beg for the return of his beloved. His music had power to move hard rocks; it might also move the cold heart of Hades. Hope gave him back his songs, and, playing and singing, he walked down the dark, steep path.

His silvery voice floated down through the dark like a gentle summer breeze and its magic moved the iron gates of Hades. They sprang open and let him in, and Cerberus, the three-headed watchdog, lay down at his feet and let him pass. The whole dark underworld stilled and listened to Orpheus' music as he entered the realm of the dead singing about his great love, begging to have his Euridice back. The fluttering souls hushed. Those condemned to eternal pains stopped groaning, and their torturers, the avenging furies, the Erinyes, dropped their whips and wept tears of blood.

Hades, the pitiless king of the dead, sat on his black marble throne with Queen Persephone at his side. Even he was so moved by the music that tears rolled down his sallow cheeks and cold Persephone sobbed. Her heart was so touched that she turned to her husband and begged him to let Euridice go back to the sunny world above. Hades gave his consent, but he made one condition: Orpheus must not look at his bride before they reached the realm of the living. She would walk behind him, but if he turned, and looked at her, she must return to the underworld.

102 Overcome with joy, Orpheus started up the dark path, and as his music faded into the distance, gloom again descended over the underworld. The way was long, and as Orpheus walked on and on, doubt began to creep into his mind. Had Hades deceived him? Were the sounds he

heard behind him really Euridice's footsteps? He had almost reached the upper world, and could already see a dim light ahead, when he could bear his doubts no longer. He had to turn and see if she really was there. He saw her sweet face, but only for an instant, for again Hermes appeared at her side. He turned her about and led her back to the dark gloom below. Faintly, Orpheus heard her whisper farewell. He had lost her forever through his lack of faith.

Orpheus never again found joy on earth. He wandered into the wilderness to grieve in solitude. He sang, but now his songs were so mournful that tears trickled down the cheeks of wild beasts and the willows wept.

A band of wild nymphs stormed through the woods shouting to Orpheus to join them. They yelled and carried on so loudly that they could not hear his silvery voice and were not touched by its magic. They wanted him to dance with them, but he had no heart for their revelry, and in a fury they threw themselves over him. They tore him to pieces and tossed his body into a river. The river stopped its gurgling to listen, for the haunting voice of Orpheus still issued forth from his dead lips as he floated down to the open sea.

The Muses grieved over him. They searched the sea till they found his body on the shores of the island of Lesbos. There they gave him a proper funeral, and at last he could rejoin his beloved Euridice as a flitting ghost in the underworld.

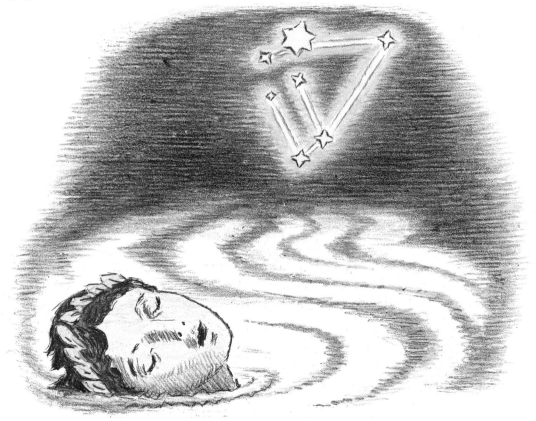

THE MUSES sang not only of the gods and of the spirits sprung from
Mother Earth, but also of great kings and heroes, descended all from

mighty Zeus. The tales of heroes and brave men still ring in our ears as
we listen to the Muses sing.

MORTAL DESCENDANTS
OF ZEUS
EUROPA AND CADMUS

JOYOUSLY the Muses sang about lovely Europa, chosen by Zeus to be the first Queen of Crete. Her father, King Agenor of Tyre, was a descendant of Io, the girl who had fled to Egypt in the shape of a white cow.

Zeus had been looking far and wide for a maiden worthy of being Queen of Crete, the island where he had been raised. One day his eyes fell on Europa, and her beauty quite captured his heart.

Changing himself into a snow-white bull, he trotted about in the meadow by the sea where Europa was playing with her maidens. At first she was afraid of the strange bull who suddenly stood beside her, but as he looked at her with big, soft eyes, she lost her fear. She tied a wreath of flowers around his broad neck and gently patted his glistening sides. The bull knelt down at her feet, and trustingly she climbed up on his back and asked him to take her for a ride. He walked up and down the beach with her, and Europa laughed and clapped her hands and called to her maidens to come and see the marvelous bull she had found. But suddenly the bull turned and rushed away over the sea with her. Her maidens cried out in terror and the king came running out of his palace, just in time to see the bull and his daughter disappear beyond the horizon.

Trembling, Europa clung to the horns of the bull. But to her surprise, not a drop of water touched her toes, for Nereids swimming all about smoothed the waves with their hands and made the sea a polished road for the bull to run on. Then the bull turned his head and spoke. He was not a bull, he said, but Zeus himself, and he had come to earth to make her his bride and the Queen of Crete.

When Zeus arrived in Crete with Europa, he put a royal crown of jewels on her head as a token of his love, and she lived in Crete in glory and delight to the end of her days. She had three sons: Minos and Sarpedon, who became great kings, and Radamanthus who was so wise that after his death he was made a judge in the underworld.

When Zeus returned to Olympus, he ordered his son Hephaestus, the smith, to make a bronze robot that would watch over Crete and Europa. Three times a day, Talos, the robot, walked with clanking steps

around the shores of the island, and whenever an enemy ship approached, he hurled rocks at it and sank it.

The king of Tyre had sent his three sons to search for their kidnaped sister. Two of the brothers soon gave up, but Cadmus, the third brother, sailed on to Greece with his men. There he went to the oracle at Delphi and asked where Europa could be found. His sister was well and happy, he was told, and he must give up the search for her. Instead, he should stay in Greece and found a new kingdom; a snow-white cow would lead him to a good site for a walled city.

Cadmus left Delphi, and indeed, before long, he met a white cow. He followed her uphill and downhill, over mountains and through valleys, and at last the cow lay down on top of a knoll in the middle of a wide plain. Cadmus saw with pleasure that it was a perfect site for a walled city. He sent one of his men for water from a nearby bubbling spring. The man did not return. Cadmus sent another man to look for him. He did not return either, and, one after another, Cadmus sent off all his men, but not one of them came back. At last, he went himself to see what had happened and found a dragon guarding the spring. The monster had devoured all his men, and now it was so sluggish and sleepy that Cadmus easily slayed it. But that did not bring his men back to life and Cadmus could not build a walled city all alone. He sacrificed the white cow to the gods and begged them for help. Athena answered his plea. "Plow a field," she told him. "Pull out the dragon's teeth and sow them in the furrows."

This advice sounded strange, but Cadmus did as he was told. As soon as the dragon's teeth were sown, up shot a host of fierce warriors. They rushed at Cadmus, waving their swords and the terror-struck hero gave himself up for lost. Again, Athena called to him: "Throw a rock among them!" He did, and at once the warriors flew at one another, each accusing his neighbor of having thrown the rock. They fought furiously till only five were left, and they were badly wounded. Cadmus nursed them back to health and they became his faithful men and helped him to build Thebes, the great walled city with seven gates.

Cadmus became a great king and the gods favored him. Zeus gave him Harmonia, a daughter of Aphrodite, for his queen. The gods gave the bride a magic necklace to keep her beautiful and young and Thebes, ruled by Cadmus and his descendants, became one of the greatest Greek cities.

TANTALUS AND PELOPS

THE MUSES sang about Tantalus, condemned to suffer forever in the underworld. He stood in water up to his neck, but could never quench his thirst, for whenever he bent to drink, the water receded. Above his head hung branches loaded with fruits, but whenever he tried to pick one, the branch bent out of his reach.

Tantalus was a son of Zeus, and he had been so favored by the gods that he had been invited to feast with them on high Olympus. In return, he had asked the gods to come to dine in his palace in Asia Minor. He was a king of vast riches, but nothing he owned seemed good enough to set before his exalted guests. His son, Pelops, was his greatest treasure, and, wanting to give the gods his best, Tantalus decided to sacrifice him. He made a stew of him and set the dish before the gods. But the Olympian gods detested human sacrifice. Outraged, they threw Tantalus to the punishing grounds in the underworld and brought Pelops back to life. But one of his shoulder bones was missing, and the gods replaced it with a piece of ivory. They all gave him rich gifts. Poseidon gave him a team of fast horses and told him to set off and win himself a new kingdom.

In Greece there was a beautiful princess whose name was Hippodamia. She was the daughter of Oenomaüs, the King of Elis, and whoever married her would inherit his kingdom, but her father loved her so dearly that he could not bear to part with her. He had a team of horses given to him by Ares, the god of war, whose son he was, and whenever a

suitor came to ask for his daughter's hand, Oenomaüs challenged him to a chariot race. If the suitor won, he would win the princess; if he lost, he would lose his head. No horses on earth could outrun the horses of Ares, and the heads of twelve suitors already hung at the gates of the palace. When Pelops arrived in Elis to woo the princess, Oenomaüs did not know that Pelops also had a team of magic horses, and the King looked forward to nailing the thirteenth head on the gates! But Hippodamia fell in love with the young prince and wanted to save his life. She asked her father's stable boy to fix the king's chariot so that Pelops would win. The stable boy, eager to please her, did more than he was asked to do. He took out the wooden pins that held the wheels to the axle, and replaced them with pins of wax.

Never had there been such a race! The fiery horses ran neck to neck, and the king, to his surprise, could not pull ahead, no matter how hard he swung the whip. Then suddenly the wax pins gave way. The wheels of the chariot flew off and the king was thrown to his death.

Pelops married Hippodamia and became the King of Elis. He flung the faithless stable boy into the sea, and gave the old king a magnificent funeral feast inviting heroes from all over Greece to take part in athletic games in his honor and offered fabulous prizes to the winners, for Pelops had brought with him the great riches of his father, Tantalus. The games were held on the plain of Olympia, in Elis, and were to be repeated every four years. They were called the Olympic games.

DANAÜS, PERSEUS, AND
THE GORGON

LOUD was the song of the Muses about Danaüs, first of a line of great kings and heroes.

King Danaüs of Libya had fifty daughters, his brother, King Aegyptus, had fifty sons. The fifty sons wanted to marry the fifty daughters, but they were rough and rowdy and King Danaüs did not want them for sons-in-law. He feared that they might carry off his daughters by force, so secretly he built a ship with fifty oars and fled with his daughters. The fifty princesses pulled at the oars and rowed the ship across the wide sea. They reached Argos, in Greece, and when the people there saw the king standing in the prow of a gorgeous ship rowed by princesses, they were awed. They were certain that Danaüs had been sent by the gods, and made him their king.

Danaüs was a good ruler, and peace and happiness reigned in Argos until one day another splendid ship arrived. And who should be at the oars but King Aegyptus' fifty sons, who had come to claim their brides. Danaüs did not dare to oppose them and had a lavish wedding feast prepared. But secretly he gave each of his fifty daughters a dagger and ordered them all to kill their husbands as soon as they were alone. Forty-nine of the brides obeyed him. But Hypermnestra, the eldest, fell in love with Lynceus, her prince, and fled with him. In vain did Danaüs try to find new husbands for his widowed daughters; nobody dared to marry them. The forty-nine Danaïdes had to live a life without joy, and when they died and came to the underworld, they were sentenced to carry water forever in sieves, trying in vain to fill a bath and wash off their sins.

When King Danaüs grew old, there was no heir to his throne, and he had to send for Hypermnestra and Lynceus, who were living in great happiness. They became King and Queen of Argos, and their son became King after them. When he died, his son, Acrisius, inherited the throne. Acrisius, however, had no son. He had only a beautiful, golden-haired daughter whose name was Danaë, but her beauty brought no joy to her father. He wanted a son and heir to his kingdom. When an oracle told him that he would die by the hand of his daughter's son, he put Danaë in a sealed chamber that had neither windows nor doors, only an opening in the roof. There no suitor could see her beauty and she would remain unwed and childless. But Acrisius forgot to reckon with Zeus. The thunder-god spied the lonesome maiden through the opening in the roof, and in the shape of a golden shower he descended to her. No longer was Danaë lonesome, for now she was the happy bride of Zeus. But when her father heard the cries of an infant from her chamber he broke through the walls in a rage, intending to kill his grandson. When he learned that Zeus was the child's father he did not dare to lay hands on him. Instead, he put Danaë and her son, Perseus, in a chest and threw it into the sea. If they drowned, Poseidon would be to blame.

115

Zeus gently steered the chest to the shore of an island, and a fisherman who was casting his nets hauled it in. Great was his surprise when he saw what the chest contained. When Danaë had told him her story, he took her and little Perseus to his hut and cared for them as if they were his own, for he was a kind old man and childless.

In his humble hut Perseus grew into a fine and valiant youth, proud of being the son of Zeus and the beautiful Danaë. But Danaë's beauty attracted the eye of the ruthless king of the island. He wanted her for his queen. In vain did Danaë turn him away. She was the bride of Zeus and swore that she could marry no other. The king pursued her and would have carried her off by force if Perseus had not protected her. The scheming king decided to get rid of Perseus, and he let it be known that he was going to marry a princess from a neighboring island. As was the custom, all the men in the kingdom brought him gifts. Only Perseus was so poor that he had nothing to give. So he offered his services to the king instead. This was just what the king had expected. "Slay the monster Medusa and bring me her head," he said. No man who had ever set out to kill Medusa had come back, and the king was sure that now he was forever rid of Perseus.

Medusa was one of three horrible Gorgon sisters, so gruesome that all living creatures turned to stone at the sight of them. They lived on an island far out at sea, but nobody knew just where.

Perseus bid his mother good-by and set out to search for Medusa. He went over land and over sea asking his way, but nobody could tell him where the Gorgons lived. As he stood at a crossroad wondering which way to go, Athena and Hermes suddenly appeared. Zeus had sent them to help him. They could tell him the way to the island of the Gorgons, but he needed more help than that. Athena lent him her shield, polished as brightly as a mirror. Hermes lent him his sword, which was so sharp that it could cut through the hardest metal, and he also needed three magic things owned by the nymphs of the north, they told him, but even the gods did not know where these nymphs lived. That was a secret closely guarded by the three Gray Sisters, and they would never willingly reveal it, for they were the Gorgons' sisters. But Hermes offered to take Perseus to them and find a way to get the secret out of them. He took Perseus under his arm, swung himself into the air, and flew off, swifter than the wind. They flew far, far to the west and at last they came to a land where the sun never shone and everything was as gray as dusk. There sat the three Gray Sisters. Their hair was gray, their faces were gray, and they had only one gray eye between them, which they took turns looking through. As one of the sisters was handing the eye to another, Perseus sprang forward and snatched it.

"Now I have your eye," cried Perseus. "You will never get it back unless you tell me the way to the nymphs of the north."

The three Gray Sisters wailed and begged for their eye, but Perseus would not give it back, and so they had to tell him the way. Again Hermes took him under his arm and flew with him far, far to the north, beyond the North Wind, where the sun never set. The nymphs of the north received them kindly, and when they heard why Perseus had come, they gladly lent him the three things he needed; a pair of winged sandals to carry him through the air, a cap to make him invisible and a magic bag to hold whatever was put into it. Now he was ready to slay the Medusa, said Hermes. He showed him the way and wished him good luck. Wearing the winged sandals, Perseus flew far to the west. When he came to the island of the Gorgons he did not look down. He looked, instead, into Athena's polished shield, and shuddered at the sight he saw mirrored there. The three Gorgon sisters were lying on the shore, fast asleep. Long yellow fangs hung from their grinning mouths, on their heads grew writhing snakes instead of hair, and their necks were covered with scales of bronze. Around them stood the strangest stones; it was easy to see that they had once been men.

Looking into the mirroring shield, Perseus swooped down, and with one deft stroke he cut off the Medusa's head. Out from the monster's severed neck sprang a beautiful winged horse, the Pegasus. He neighed and the other two Gorgons awoke. Quickly Perseus threw Medusa's head into the magic bag and swung himself into the air. Wailing, the two Gorgon sisters took to the air on heavy wings in groping pursuit. They could not find him, for he had put on the magic cap of invisibility.

On his way home, as he flew over the coast of Ethiopia, Perseus saw, far below, a beautiful maiden chained to a rock by the sea. She was so pale that at first he thought she was a marble statue, but then he saw tears trickling from her eyes. He swooped down and tore at her chains, trying to break them.

"Flee!" she said. "Or you too will be devoured by the sea monster!" But Perseus refused to leave and she told her sad story: Her name was Andromeda and she was the daughter of King Cepheus and Queen Cassiopeia. Her mother was very vain and had boasted unwisely that she was even lovelier than the Nereids. Poseidon could not tolerate having a mortal compare herself to the goddesses of the sea, and as punishment he sent a sea monster to ravage the kingdom of Ethiopia. To appease the angry god and save his kingdom, her father had to sacrifice her, his only

daughter, to the monster. And there she stood, chained to the cliff, waiting to be devoured. She had begged the prince to whom she was engaged to save her, but he had fled in fear.

"I shall save you and you shall be mine," said Perseus.

As he spoke, a horrible sea monster came from the sea, its huge mouth opened wide to swallow Andromeda. But Perseus sprang into the air, dived at the monster and drove his sword deep into its throat. The monster bellowed, lashed its tail wildly, and rolled over on its back. It sank and the sea was tinted red by its blood. Ever since, that stretch of water has been called the Red Sea.

No sooner was the monster dead than Andromeda's cowardly suitor returned with many warriors to claim her for his bride. Now he was bold and menacing and King Cepheus did not dare to oppose him.

"Andromeda, shield your eyes!" cried Perseus, and with that he lifted the head of the Medusa out of the bag. The suitor and his men stared in horror and whips!, they were changed into stones! Unfortunately, the king and the queen had also looked at the Gorgon's head and they too turned into stone. But since a son of Zeus was going to marry their daughter, the gods took pity on them and hung Cepheus and Cassiopeia in the sky as constellations.

Perseus lifted Andromeda into his arms and flew homewards. But when he arrived at the fisherman's hut, he learned that Danaë and the fisherman had gone into hiding. As soon as the king of the island had gotten rid of Perseus, he had tried to carry Danaë off. To save her, the kind old fisherman had fled with her. When Perseus heard that, he made straight for the king's palace.

"Here is the head you wanted!" he shouted, and pulled Medusa's head out of the bag. Startled, the king and his men looked up, and there they sat, turned into statues of stone, some of them with their mouths still open in astonishment.

The people of the island rejoiced at being rid of the tyrant, and as soon as the fisherman and Danaë came out of hiding, they made the fisherman their new king. He gave Perseus and Andromeda the grandest of wedding feasts and everybody was happy.

Perseus did not keep the Gorgon's head, it was much too dangerous for a mortal to own. He gave it to Athena when he returned her shield and the other magic objects he had borrowed.

Perseus thought that his grandfather Acrisius would be happy to see him now that he was a hero, and he set sail for Argos with Danaë and Andromeda. But when the old king learned that his grandson was approaching he fled, for he still remembered the oracle's warning, and so Perseus became king of Argos.

Perseus ruled wisely and well, his mother and his wife always at his side. Since he was a great athlete, he also took part in games all over Greece. One day, a sudden gust of wind changed the course of a discus he had thrown, and it killed an old man who was watching the games. Who should that old man be but Acrisius, his grandfather! Thus the words of the oracle came true.

After that, Perseus no longer wanted to live in his grandfather's city, Argos. So he founded instead the splendid fortified city of Mycenae, not far away, and many great kings and heroes were descended from him and Andromeda.

When at last Perseus and Andromeda died, Zeus put them, too, in the sky as constellations.

CLEVER AND
VAINGLORIOUS KINGS

WHEN PERSEUS gave Athena the Gorgon's head, she fastened it on her breastplate, and it made her still more powerful. She also fetched two of Medusa's bones, and from them she made herself a double flute. She could not understand why Hera and Aphrodite burst out laughing every time she played on it, for she was very pleased with the music she made. But one day she saw her own image in her polished shield. With puckered lips and puffed cheeks she did not look at all like her stately self. In disgust she threw the flute down to earth and put a curse on it.

Marsyas, a satyr who was capering about in the Phrygian woods, found the flute and began to play on it. When he discovered he could play two melodies at the same time, he was wild with joy. He hopped through the woods, playing on his double flute, boasting that now he could make better music than Apollo himself.

Apollo frowned when he heard that a satyr dared compare himself to him, the god of music, and he stormed down from Olympus to the Phrygian woods. He found Marsyas who was so delighted with his own music that he even challenged Apollo to a contest.

"You shall have your contest," said Apollo, "but if I win, you shall lose your hide."

The nine Muses, of course, were to be the judges, and Marsyas insisted that King Midas of Phrygia also be a judge.

123

KING MIDAS was a kind but rather stupid man who had always
been a friend to the Phrygian satyrs. One morning his servants had found
an old satyr sleeping in the king's favorite flower bed. Midas had spared the
satyr from punishment and let him go. This old satyr was a follower of
Dionysus, and the god had rewarded Midas for his kindness by granting
him a wish. Shortsightedly, King Midas wished that everything he touched
would turn to gold. His golden touch made him the richest man on earth,
but he almost starved to death for even his food and drink turned to gold.
And when his little daughter ran to him to hug him, she too turned into
gold! Midas had to beg Dionysus to undo his wish and make everything as
it had been before.

Now again, King Midas showed poor judgment. The nine Muses all
agreed that Apollo was by far the better musician, but Midas voted for
the Phrygian satyr. Apollo disdainfully turned his lyre upside down and
played just as well as before. He ordered Marsyas to turn his flute and
do the same. Not a sound came from Marsyas' flute however hard he
blew, and even Midas had to admit that the satyr's flute was inferior to

Apollo's lyre. So Marsyas lost the contest and Apollo pulled off his skin and made a drum of it. Then he turned to King Midas and said, "Ears as stupid as yours belong to an ass. Ass's ears you shall have from now on!"

Ever after, King Midas went about with a tall, peaked cap on his head to hide his long ears. His subjects thought he had started a new fashion, and it wasn't long before all the Phrygians wore tall, peaked caps.

The king's barber was the only one who knew what Midas was hiding. He had been forbidden to breathe a word about it and he almost burst from having to keep such an important secret. When he could bear it no longer he ran out to a lonesome field, dug a hole in the ground, and whispered into it, "King Midas has ass's ears!" He quickly covered up the hole and thought the secret was safe. But the nearby reeds had heard and as they swayed in the wind they whispered, "Midas has ass's ears, Midas has ass's ears," and soon the secret spread all over the world.

King Midas was so ashamed that he left his throne and hid deep in the woods where no one could see him.

Sisyphus of Corinth was the cleverest king who ever lived. He was so cunning that he fooled even the gods.

One day Sisyphus saw the river-god Asopus, who was looking for his daughter, Aegina. Sisyphus, who noticed everything that was happening in his kingdom, went after him and said, "I'll tell you what has become of your daughter if you'll give my city a spring." For the only thing his great city lacked was a good supply of fresh water.

Asopus hated to part with any of his water. He twisted and squirmed, but at last he struck the ground, and a crystal clear spring bubbled forth.

"It is Zeus himself who has carried off your daughter," said Sisyphus. "I saw him hurry by with her," and he pointed out to Asopus the way Zeus had taken. The river-god rushed off in a fury and soon caught up with the elopers. Zeus, taken by surprise, had no thunderbolt at hand, so, to save himself and the nymph from the river-god's rage, he changed himself into a rock and her into the island Aegina.

Sisyphus had his spring of water, but Asopus lost his daughter, and Zeus was furious with Sisyphus for meddling in his affairs. He asked Hades to take him to the underworld and punish him severely. Hades

126

was glad to do his brother Zeus a favor and he went himself to fetch Sisyphus. When the sly king saw the lord of the dead in person, he pretended to be very honored. But why, he asked, had not Hermes, whose office it was to guide dead souls to the underworld, come for him? While Hades searched for a suitable answer, Sisyphus deftly wound a chain around him. And there stood the lord of the dead, chained to a post like a dog.

As long as Sisyphus kept Hades tied up, nobody could die. The Fates got the threads of life tangled and the whole world was in confusion. Finally the gods threatened to make life so miserable for Sisyphus that he would wish he were dead, and Sisyphus then had to let Hades go. Again people could die and life could go on normally. The very first soul to be claimed was, of course, that of Sisyphus himself. This time Hermes came for him. The wily king, who had expected this, had told his loving wife not to give him a funeral feast, and not to put a coin under his tongue. So he arrived in the realm of the dead as a poor beggar. Hades was shocked! After all, Sisyphus was a king and entitled to a funeral feast and a golden coin under his tongue to pay for his passage across the Styx. His wife had to be punished, or she might set a bad example for others. He sent Sisyphus back to earth and told him to teach his wife respect. "Fooled him again!" said Sisyphus when he rejoined his devoted wife. They lived happily for many long years, till at last he died of old age and went to Hades for good. There he was given a task that kept him too busy to think up new tricks. He had to push a boulder up a steep hill, but every time he had almost reached the top, the boulder slipped from his hands and rolled all the way to the bottom again.

Bellerophon, a grandson of Sisyphus, was a great tamer of horses. He would have given all he owned for a ride on the winged horse Pegasus, who had sprung out of Medusa's neck. Pegasus had flown to Greece, where the nine Muses had found him and tended him. They were the only ones who could come close enough to touch him, for Pegasus was wild and swift.

One night, Bellerophon fell asleep in Athena's temple. He dreamed that the goddess gave him a golden bridle that would make the flying horse tame. And when he awoke, he really held a golden bridle in his hand.

Not long thereafter, Pegasus flew over Corinth, saw the clear spring that Sisyphus had won from the river-god, and stopped to drink. Carefully Bellerophon tiptoed up to the winged horse and flung the bridle over his head. The horse neighed, looked at Bellerophon, and suddenly he was so tame that Bellerophon could mount him. Never had there been such a horse and such a horseman. They galloped through the air, over land and over sea, faster than the wind.

On the back of his flying horse, Bellerophon set off to fight the Chimera, a fire-breathing beast that was ravaging the kingdom of Lycia in Asia Minor. The Chimera was more fearful than a nightmare. She was lion in front, serpent in back, and goat in between. She spat fire from all her three heads and her hide was so tough that no weapon could pierce it. Swooping down as close as he dared without singeing the coat of his flying horse, Bellerophon went at the monster with a lump of lead stuck to the end of his spear. The Chimera hissed like a serpent, bleated like a goat, and as she opened wide her lion's jaws to roar, he thrust the lump of lead down her throat. Her flaming breath melted the lead and it trickled into her stomach and killed her.

The people of Lycia, who had been hiding in fear behind bolted doors, now dared to come out, and the king of the country was so thankful that he gave Bellerophon the hand of his daughter. When the old king died, Bellerophon inherited the kingdom. He became a great king, loved by his people, feared by his neighbors and all the monsters lurking nearby. But his fame went to his head and he grew so vain that he thought he was as great as the gods. He even held himself equal to Zeus. He soared ever higher on his flying horse, and at last he tried to enter Olympus itself. There pride took a spill. Pegasus threw him and Bellerophon fell to earth, landing in thistle thorns in a distant country. Torn and lame, he wandered about as an unknown beggar until he died. Pegasus entered Olympus alone and Zeus made the handsome winged horse the carrier of his thunderbolts.

MELAMPUS, a cousin of Bellerophon, won glory and fame and one third of a kingdom, all because he was kind to animals. Once when he was a child, he found a dead mother snake on the road. He did not kick it into a ditch, but gave it a proper funeral, picked up the little motherless snakes, and reared them tenderly. In gratitude they licked his ears so clean that he could understand the language of all animals, crawling and flying. From their talk he learned the secrets of the earth and grew wise beyond measure.

Once he was thrown into prison for trying to steal some cows from a neighboring king, and one night as he lay on his cot, he heard a family of termites talking inside the roof beam. "Brother," said one termite to another, "if we go on chewing all night, the roof will collapse before morning."

Melampus jumped up and hammered at the door. He demanded to be moved at once, for the roof would soon fall in. The jailer laughed, but Melampus made such a fuss that he was finally moved. Just then the roof did cave in. Everybody marveled, and the king called for him and told him that, if he could find a cure for his sick son, he could have the cows he had tried to steal. The young prince had been sick since he was a child, and no one knew what ailed him.

Melampus slaughtered an ox and spread the meat on the ground. Right away, two vultures swooped down and began to gorge themselves. When they had eaten their fill, one of the vultures said to the other, "I haven't been so full since that time when the king sacrificed a ram to the gods. I remember how terrified the little prince was when he saw his father with a bloody knife in his hand. He screamed so loudly that his father threw away his knife and ran to comfort him. The knife stuck in the tree over yonder and wounded the tree nymph. She cast a spell on the boy and he has been sick ever since. Now the bark has closed over the knife, but if the king knew what I know, he would dig out the rusty blade, make a brew from the rust, and give it to the prince to drink."

Melampus at once dug out the blade and made a rusty brew. The sickly prince drank it and right away he was so fit that he bounded over a field of barley without bending a stalk. Melampus won great fame as a healer and from all corners of Greece, kings sent for him to cure their sick.

The King of Tiryns had three lovely daughters who suddenly went quite out of their minds and thought they were cows. The king sent for Melampus, who said that he would cure them if the king would give him a third of his kingdom. That was far too much, thought the king, and Melampus went away. The princesses grew worse and ran all over the kingdom mooing like cows. The king again sent for Melampus. This time Melampus came with his brother and now he wanted a third of the kingdom for his brother, too! The king had to agree, for it was very embarrassing to him that his daughters ran around shouting, "We are cows, we are cows!"

Melampus hired some fast runners and sent them after the crazy girls. They had to run halfway across Greece before they could catch them and bring them back. Melampus forced them to drink a draught of magic herbs, and that cured all of them except one, poor girl, who died of exhaustion.

The king, who had to part with two-thirds of his kingdom, thought that he might as well give Melampus and his brother each a princess in the bargain, and they all lived happily thereafter.

131

HERACLES

PROUDLY did the Muses sing of Heracles, often called Hercules, the strongest man who ever lived on earth and the greatest of all the descendants of Danaüs. His mother was Princess Alcmena, granddaughter of Perseus and Andromeda, and famed for her beauty and virtue.

His father was Zeus, so Hera, of course, hated Alcmena and pursued Heracles with her wrath. When he was an infant the goddess sent two spotted serpents into his cradle, but little Heracles simply grasped them in his powerful hands and squeezed the life out of them. He grew stronger every day, but his trouble was that he did not know his own strength.

Being of noble birth, he had to learn to sing and play the lyre, but Heracles would much rather wrestle and fight. One day his music teacher Linus scolded him for singing out of tune. In a fit of fury Heracles banged his lyre over the teacher's head, harder than he had meant, and the blow killed the poor man. Heracles was too strong to have around a palace so he was sent into the mountains as a shepherd. There he could use his tremendous strength on prowling beasts. Soon he had rid the countryside around Thebes of lions and wolves, and the fame of his strength spread far and wide. He came back from the mountains as a hero, and the King of Thebes regarded him so highly that he gave him his daughter in marriage. Hera did not like this at all, and she made Heracles insane. Raving mad, he swatted down his own children, mistaking them for wild beasts. When he regained his senses, he was horrified at what he had done, and went to the oracle of Delphi to learn what he must do to atone for his crime. He was told that he must serve for ten years as the slave of his cousin Eurystheus and perform ten labors for him.

Hera was pleased, for Eurystheus, the King of Mycenae, was a weak little man who hated his strong cousin Heracles. With her help the king would surely think of the hardest tasks for Heracles to perform.

For his first four labors Eurystheus sent Heracles to rid the nearby countryside of dangerous beasts and monsters.

In the valley of Nemea dwelt a monstrous lion whose hide was so tough it could not be pierced by any weapons. It was one of Echidna's dreadful offspring, which Zeus had let live as a challenge to future heroes.

Heracles chased it out of its lair, seized it in his bare hands, and

squeezed it to death. Then he skinned the beast with its own claws, and with the impenetrable skin of the Nemean lion slung over his head and shoulders, he reported back to Eurystheus, his first labor performed.

In the swamps of Lerna there lived a nine-headed Hydra, another of Echidna's brood. This monster was so poisonous that the fumes from its breath alone were enough to kill whatever came close to it.

Heracles filled his enormous lungs with air, held his breath, and ran at the Hydra. Swinging his club, he knocked off its heads, and one after the other they rolled to the ground. But no sooner had he knocked off one head than a new one grew in its place. He half turned around and let out enough air to call to his charioteer to bring a firebrand and sear the necks. Then no new heads could sprout. When Hera saw that Heracles was winning over the Hydra, she sent a giant crab to pinch his heel. With a mighty kick Heracles sent the giant crab flying as he knocked off the last of the heads. Then he dipped his arrows in the Hydra's blood, making them so poisonous that a mere scratch from them was deadly, and he returned to Mycenae, his second labor performed.

On the slopes of Mount Erymanthus roamed a wild and dreadful boar, with tusks as sharp as swords. Eurystheus sent Heracles to bring this beast back alive.

With loud yells, Heracles chased the boar out of its lair and drove it ahead of him all the way to the top of the snow-capped mountain. The heavy beast sank into the snow and it was easy for Heracles to catch and subdue it. He pushed, dragged, and rolled it all the way down to the gates of Mycenae. When Eurystheus saw the fearful boar, he dived into an urn and barely dared to peek out.

Then Eurystheus sent Heracles to rid the Stymphalian Lake of a swarm of dangerous birds. They had feathers of brass so sharp that, when one of them fell to the ground, it killed whomever it hit. But they could not penetrate Heracles' lion skin, and he made such a din, with a huge rattle, that the birds took fright and flew away, never to return.

Eurystheus was distressed to see with what great ease Heracles had performed his first four labors. Now he sent him to bring back alive one of the sacred hinds of Artemis. He hoped that Heracles would harm the creature with his brute strength and thereby earn the wrath of the goddess. But Heracles pursued the swift deer with great patience over hills and dales. The year was almost over when at last he caught the deer. With great care he carried it back to Mycenae.

Next, to humble his strong cousin, Eurystheus ordered Heracles to clean the stables of King Augeas, who lived across the mountains to the west. King Augeas had huge herds and his stables and barnyards had not been cleaned for years. Heaps of dung rose mountain high. No man alive could clean his stables in a year, thought Eurystheus. But Heracles with tremendous strength changed the course of two rivers. The waters flooded through stables and barnyards and washed them clean in less than a day.

Eurystheus now, on the advice of Hera, sent Heracles far afield for his last four labors. He must travel way to the east and fetch back to Mycenae the golden girdle of Hippolyta, Queen of the Amazons. The Amazons were a tribe of wild and warlike women who rode better and fought harder than any men. Eurystheus was sure that even Heracles would be overwhelmed by the furious women. But when Heracles arrived in Amazon land, the proud queen was so taken by the sight of his bulging muscles that she gave him her belt without a fight. She would gladly

have given him her hand in the bargain, but Hera, in the disguise of an Amazon, spread the rumor that Heracles had come to kidnap Hippolyta. The Amazons threw themselves upon Heracles, but for once they had found their master! Heracles swung his mighty club, and the little Amazon husbands, who were spinning and cooking and tending the babies, were amazed to see their dangerous wives subdued by a single man.

In triumph, Heracles returned to Mycenae with Hippolyta's belt. He could not bring the queen, she had been killed in the fight.

137

Far to the north there lived a king whose name was Diomedes. He was a very inhospitable king and had trained his four mares to devour all strangers who came to his land.

Now Eurystheus sent Heracles to capture the four man-eating mares and bring them back alive.

Heracles traveled to the north, slew King Diomedes, and threw him to his own mares. When the mares had eaten the evil king, they were so tame that they let Heracles drive them back to the gates of Mycenae.

Then Eurystheus sent Heracles south to catch a fierce, fire-breathing bull on the island of Crete. The Cretans, who were great bullfighters, could not catch the bull, but Heracles seized the charging bull by the horns without heeding the flames from its nostrils, flung it to the ground, and returned to Mycenae, bringing the subdued beast. Eurystheus was glad he had a safe urn to hide in.

For his tenth labor, Heracles was sent to an island far out in the ocean, to bring back a huge herd of red cows. They belonged to Geryon, a monster with three bodies on one pair of legs.

Heracles walked off with a powerful stride and soon reached the end of all land in the west. The only boat he could spot was the golden vessel of Helios, the sun. Heracles aimed his mighty bow at the sun and threatened to shoot him from the sky if he did not lend it to him. Helios did not dare to refuse, and he let Heracles take his golden boat.

Before he sailed off, Heracles pulled up two huge crags and set them down, one on each side of the strait that separates Europe from Africa. There they stand to this day, called the Pillars of Hercules.

When Heracles was out at sea and the waves rose high around him, he aimed a poisoned arrow at the waves, threatening to shoot them if they did not still at once. The waves flattened in fear and Heracles sailed on to Geryon's island. He began at once to load the herd of red cows, and Geryon's watchman and his two-headed dog rushed at him. With one swing of his mighty club Heracles did away with them both. Then Geryon himself came running to attack him, his three huge bodies swaying on his thin legs. Calmly Heracles lifted his bow, took careful aim, and sent a poisoned arrow through all of the monster's three bodies. As time was getting short, Heracles rowed back as fast as he could with the herd. When he arrived at the mainland, Hera sent a swarm of gadflies to sting the cows and they scattered all over Europe. Still, Heracles man-

aged to round them up and bring them to the gates of Mycenae just before the year was up. There, Eurystheus sacrificed the cows to Hera, and, gratified, the goddess whispered into his ear that he must demand two more labors from Heracles, for his charioteer had helped him to singe the heads of the Hydra, and not he but the waters of two rivers had washed the Augean stables clean.

Heracles scowled but he bowed his head in submission, for he had won much glory on his ten labors and hoped to win some more.

For his eleventh labor, Heracles was sent to find Hera's secret garden of the Hesperides and pick three golden apples from the little apple tree that Mother Earth had given Hera for her wedding gift. Nereus, the Old Gray Man of the Sea, was the only one on earth who knew where the garden was, but he would not reveal the secret. When Heracles seized him to squeeze the secret out of him, Nereus tried to escape by changing himself into all kinds of animals. But Heracles held on to him and at last Nereus had to tell him that the garden of the Hesperides lay west of the setting sun, not far from where the Titan Atlas stood, holding up the sky.

On his way to the garden, Heracles heard the groans of the Titan Prometheus, who was chained to the Caucasus Mountains. Heracles was in a hurry, but he felt sorry for the Titan and took time off to tear apart his chains. Zeus, impressed by the strength of his son, let him do it. In gratitude Prometheus warned Heracles not to pick the golden apples himself, or he would die. They were apples of immortality and could be picked only by a god.

139

Heracles traveled over land and over sea, and at last he came to the garden of the Hesperides. Nearby stood the Titan Atlas, and Heracles offered to hold up the sky for him if he would pick three golden apples from Hera's tree. Atlas said he would be glad to be rid of his heavy burden for a while, but he feared the dragon Ladon, which lay under the tree watching it with all the eyes of his hundred heads. A hundred-headed dragon could not frighten Heracles. He drew his bow and shot it. Then he took the sky on his shoulders, and Atlas reached out and picked the apples. The three little nymphs who tended the tree wept bitter tears, but they could not stop Atlas, now that the watchful dragon was dead.

Heracles' knees started to buckle, so heavy was the weight of the sky, but Atlas stretched himself, enjoying his freedom.

"I might as well take these apples to Eurystheus myself," said the Titan, and started to walk away. Heracles well understood that Atlas had no intention of ever coming back, but he pretended to agree.

"Very well," he said, "just hold the sky while I make a pad of my lion skin, the sky is hard on my shoulders."

This sounded reasonable to Atlas. He put down the golden apples and braced himself against the vault of the sky.

"Thank you for picking the apples," said Heracles, and hurried homeward.

On his way to Mycenae, Heracles was stopped by the giant wrestler Antaeus. He lived in a hut beside the road, and forced all travelers to wrestle with him. He was a son of Mother Earth and could not die as long as he touched her, so he always won and had built his hut of the skulls and bones of his victims. When Heracles threw the giant to the ground, thinking he was dead, but saw him springing up revived, he understood what was happening. Seizing Antaeus, he held him in the air until he had squeezed all life out of him.

Heracles hurried on to Mycenae and gave the golden apples to Eurystheus. But Eurystheus did not dare to keep them. He gave them to Athena, who took them back to Hera's garden, where they belonged.

For his twelfth labor Heracles had to go to the underworld, capture
140 Cerberus, the snarling, three-headed watchdog of Hades, and bring him to Mycenae.

Heracles searched far and wide till at last he found an entrance to the underworld near Helios' evening palace, far to the west. Setting his

face in a terrible scowl, he walked straight down to Hades. The fluttering souls trembled and Hades himself was so frightened at the sight that he told him to take the dog, only please not to treat it too roughly. Cerberus growled and lashed out with his spiked tail, but Heracles threw his arms around him and squeezed him till the dog's three tongues hung out. Whining, Cerberus let Heracles drag him to the upper world and all the way to the gates of Mycenae. When Eurystheus saw the fearful hound, once again he dived into the urn and cowered there, not daring to make a sound. Heracles did not know what to do with the dog, so he dragged Cerberus all the way back down to Hades.

Now Heracles was free. He had performed not only ten but twelve labors. He had atoned for his sins and Zeus was very pleased with his strong son. He was pleased with Hera, too, for she had unknowingly helped Heracles win more glory and fame than any other hero on earth. Admired by everyone, Heracles traveled all over Greece, performing more heroic deeds and making many friends.

But Hera, still relentless, again made him insane and he swatted men down like flies. When he recovered his senses, he once more had to atone for his sins, and this time it was his father, Zeus, who meted out his punishment, seeing to it that there was no glory to be won.

Zeus sentenced Heracles to serve for three years as the slave of Queen Omphale of Lydia. She dressed him in woman's clothes and made the strongest man in the world sit at her feet, spinning and sewing with his huge hands, while she herself donned his lion skin and brandished his club. Heracles grumbled and groaned, but he did as he was ordered. When his three years at last were over, he had learned his lesson of humility.

Again he performed heroic deeds and his friends were glad to see him back. One of his great friends was Admetus, King of Thessaly, under whom Apollo once had served when he was a slave on earth. To thank Admetus for his kindness, Apollo had persuaded the Fates not to cut his thread of life when his time to die had come, as long as Admetus could find someone else willing to die in his stead. That would be easy, thought the king. His faithful men were always saying that his life was dearer to them than their own. King Admetus had always been afraid of dying early, for he was very happy with his beautiful queen, Alcestis. The king and the queen were both fond of Heracles and always welcomed him

warmly. But one day when Heracles came to the palace, King Admetus greeted him alone. He looked sad and downcast. When Heracles asked him what was wrong, he said nothing except that a woman of the household had died and he must go to her funeral. And he left Heracles alone with the servants. They too looked sad. They waited on him in silence and did not answer his questions. Heracles ate, drank, and made merry alone and at last he grew impatient, grasped one of the servants, and forced him to speak. The servant told him that the time had come for Admetus to die, and he had turned to his men and asked one of them to die in his stead. But now not one of them had been willing. Admetus then went to his parents, who were old and weary of life, and asked them to die in his stead. They too refused. But when he returned to his palace, he found Queen Alcestis setting off for the realm of the dead. She loved him so much, she said, she would gladly give her life for him, and the king was so fond of his own life that he let his queen depart. Now the king and all the household were mourning for Alcestis.

144 Heracles shed big tears when he heard this sad story, but, being a man of action, he seized his club and strode off to the underworld to force Hades to give Alcestis back. Such a loving wife should not be allowed to die.

Heracles did not have to use his club. Cerberus slunk out of the way

as he stormed into the palace of Hades. The lord of the dead, himself, had a cold, unloving queen and he was so moved when Heracles told him of Alcestis' devotion that he let her go.

Heracles brought Queen Alcestis back to King Admetus and the grief in the palace changed to great joy. Now they all ate, drank, and made merry together and Alcestis grew famous far and wide as the most devoted wife who ever lived.

Heracles too wanted a wife and he chose Deianira, a Caledonian princess, for his bride. Deianira had already been promised to the river-god Achelous, but she dreaded the thought of being married to a river-god, who could change his shape at will. She would never know in which shape her husband would come home at night. She would rather marry the great hero Heracles. The two suitors agreed to wrestle, the victor to have the Princess Deianira. Of course, Heracles won. The river-god rushed at him in the shape of a bull, and Heracles seized him by a horn, wrenched it off, and threw him to the ground before he had time to change into something else. So Heracles and Deianira were married and were very happy together.

One day as they were out traveling, they came to a swollen stream. Heracles forded it with ease, but Deianira was afraid and stood on the bank. Along came the centaur Nessus and politely offered to carry her

145

across. But Nessus, like all centaurs, was fond of pretty girls and before he had reached midstream he had made up his mind to carry her off. Once on the other side, he galloped off with her. Deianira screamed for help, Heracles shot a poisoned arrow at the centaur and Nessus fell to the ground. Before he died he whispered to Deianira, "Take some of my blood and save it. If you ever fear that you are losing your husband's love, paint some of the blood on his tunic and he will love you again."

Deianira carefully saved the drops of blood, for she knew well that many a girl would like to steal her magnificent husband.

One day as Heracles was away at war, he won a great victory and sent a messenger home for his best tunic. He wanted to celebrate with his men, but Deianira thought he wanted to make himself handsome for a girl. She painted some of Nessus' blood on the tunic. As soon as Heracles put it on, he felt as though a thousand fires were burning him. It was not a love potion that Nessus had given Deianira, but the deadly poison of the Hydra from Heracles' arrow, mixed with Nessus' blood. Heracles was so strong that the poison could not kill him, but his sufferings were unbearable. He ordered his men to build a funeral pyre, spread his lion skin over the top, and lay down on it. Then he gave his bow and deadly arrows to his young friend, Philoctetes, as a parting gift. As the flames rose around him, a loud thunderclap was heard, and Heracles, by the order of Zeus, rose up to Olympus, reclining on his lion skin.

The gods all welcomed Heracles and were glad to have him with them, for the Fates had predicted that Olympus would be attacked by a fearful enemy and the Olympians could be saved only if the strongest man ever born fought on their side. The prediction soon came to pass. In a last effort to defeat the mighty thunder-god Zeus, Mother Earth had given birth to fifty snake-legged giants, who surrounded Olympus and tried to storm the palace. They seemed unconquerable, for, like Antaeus, whom Heracles had fought on earth, they sprang up again revived as soon as they touched Mother Earth. Heracles knew what to do, and with his help the gods won over the giants and cast them down into the dismal pit of Tartarus. Heracles was now the hero of Mount Olympus, beloved by all the gods. Even Hera begged him to forgive her and gave him her daughter Hebe, goddess of eternal youth, for his Olympian bride. From then on Heracles lived in eternal bliss, forever a joy to the gods. His father Zeus was very pleased.

THESEUS

THE MUSES sang of Heracles and his labors, and they also sang of the island of Crete, ruled by King Minos, the son of Zeus and Europa. His queen, Pasiphaë, a daughter of the sun-god Helios, had a golden glimmer in her eyes like all the descendants of the sun, and was accustomed to great magnificence. King Minos wanted his queen to live in a palace as splendid as her father's, and he ordered Daedalus, an Athenian architect and inventor of marvelous skill, to build the great palace of Cnossus.

The palace rose up story upon story, over a forest of columns. Winding stairs and intricate passageways connected the many halls and courtyards. Pictures were painted on the walls of the great halls, fountains splashed in the courtyards, and the bathrooms even had running water. Bulls' horns of the purest gold crowned the roofs, for the Cretans worshiped the bull, since Zeus, in the shape of a bull, had brought Europa to the island. Here the king and the queen and all their court lived in great splendor and happiness until one day Poseidon sent a snow-white bull from the sea. Since the island of Crete was completely surrounded by his domain, the sea, he too wanted to be honored, and ordered King Minos to sacrifice the bull to him. But Queen Pasiphaë was so taken by the beauty of the white bull that she persuaded the king to let it live. She admired the bull so much that she ordered Daedalus to construct a hollow wooden cow, so she could hide inside it and enjoy the beauty of the bull at close range.

Poseidon was very angry, and for punishment he made the bull mad. It ravaged the whole island, and though the Cretans were great bull-fighters, no one could subdue the beast until Heracles had come to capture it for one of his labors.

To punish the king and queen, Poseidon caused Pasiphaë to give birth to a monster, the Minotaur. He was half man, half bull, and ate nothing but human flesh. Such a fearful monster could not go free, and the clever Daedalus constructed for him a labyrinth under the palace. It was a maze of passageways and little rooms from which nobody could ever hope to find his way out. There the Minotaur was shut in, and as long as he was provided with victims to devour, he kept quiet. When he was hungry, he bellowed so loudly that the whole palace shook. King Minos had to wage war with the neighboring islands so he could supply the Minotaur with the prisoners of war for food. When a son of Minos visited Athens and was accidently killed, King Minos used this as an excuse to threaten to sack the city unless seven Athenian maidens and seven Athenian youths were sent to Crete to be sacrificed to the Minotaur every nine years.

To save his city, Aegeus, the King of Athens, had to consent, for Minos was much stronger than he. The people of Athens grumbled, for, while King Aegeus was childless and had nothing to lose, they had to see their sons and daughters sacrificed to the cruel Minotaur.

Two times nine years had passed and the king was growing old. For the third time a ship with black sails of mourning was due to depart, when word came to the king that a young hero, Theseus, from Troezen, was making his way to Athens, destroying all the monsters and high-waymen he met on the road. When King Aegeus heard that, his old heart beat faster. Once in his youth he had visited Troezen and had been secretly married to Princess Aethra. He did not bring Aethra back to Athens with him, but before he left, he said to her, "Should you bear me a son and should he grow up strong enough to lift this boulder under which I hide my sword and golden sandals, send him to me, for then he will be the worthy heir to the throne of Athens." King Aegeus in those days was known for his great strength.

Theseus, the young hero, arrived in Athens and went straight to the king's palace. Tall and handsome, he stood before Aegeus with the sandals and the sword, and the king was overjoyed. At last he had a son who was a hero as well. The king happily proclaimed Theseus the rightful heir to the throne of Athens and he became the hero of all Athens when he offered to take the place of one of the victims who were to be sent to Crete. Old King Aegeus begged his son not to go, but Theseus would not change his mind. "I shall make an end of the Minotaur and we shall return safely," he said. "We sail with black sails, but we shall return with white sails as a signal of my success."

The ship sailed to Crete and the fourteen young Athenians were locked in a dungeon to await their doom. But King Minos had a lovely daughter, Ariadne, as fair a maiden as eyes could see. She could not bear the thought that handsome Theseus should be sacrificed to the ugly Minotaur. She went to Daedalus and begged for help to save him. He gave Ariadne a magic ball of thread and told her that at midnight, when the Minotaur was fast asleep, she must take Theseus to the labyrinth. The magic ball of thread would roll ahead of him through the maze and lead him to the monster, and then it was up to Theseus to overpower the beast.

In the dark of the night, Ariadne went to Theseus' prison and whispered that, if he would promise to marry her and carry her away with him, she would help him. Gladly Theseus gave his word, and Ariadne led him to the gate of the labyrinth, tied the end of the thread to the gate so he would find his way back, and gave him the ball. As soon as Theseus put the ball of thread on the ground, it rolled ahead of him through dark corridors, up stairs, down stairs, and around winding passageways. Holding on to the unwinding thread, Theseus followed it wherever it led him, and before long he heard the thunderous snoring of the Minotaur, and there, surrounded by skulls and bleached bones, lay the monster fast asleep.

150   Theseus sprang at the Minotaur. It roared so loudly that the whole palace of Cnossus shook, but the monster was taken by surprise, and so strong was Theseus that, with his bare hands, he killed the cruel Minotaur.

Theseus quickly followed the thread back to Ariadne, who stood watch at the gate. Together they freed the other Athenians and ran to their ship in the harbor. Before they sailed, they bored holes in all of King Minos' ships so he could not pursue them. Ariadne urged them to hurry, for even she could not save them from Talos, the bronze robot who guarded the island. If he should see their ship leaving, he would throw rocks at it and sink it. Should one of them manage to swim ashore, Talos would throw himself into a blazing bonfire until he was red hot. Then he would burn the survivor to ashes in a fiery embrace. They could already hear his clanking steps, when just in time they hoisted their sail and a brisk wind blew them out to sea. In their rush they forgot to hoist the white sail of victory instead of the black sail of mourning.

Theseus' heart was filled with joy. Not only had he saved the Athenians from the Minotaur, he was also bringing a beautiful bride home to Athens. But in the middle of the night the god Dionysus appeared to him and spoke: "I forbid you to marry Ariadne. I myself have chosen her for my bride. You must set her ashore on the island of Naxos."

Theseus could not oppose an Olympian god. When they came to Naxos, he ordered everyone to go ashore and rest. There Ariadne fell into a heavy slumber, and while she slept, Theseus led the others back to the ship and they sailed off without her.

Poor Ariadne wept bitterly when she awoke and found herself deserted. Little did she suspect that the handsome stranger who came walking toward her was the god Dionysus and that it was he who had ordered

Theseus to abandon her. The god gently dried her tears and gave her a drink from the cup in his hand and right away the sadness left her. She smiled up at the god and he put a crown of sparkling jewels on her head and made her his bride. They lived happily together for many years and their sons became kings of the surrounding islands. Dionysus loved Ariadne greatly, and when she died he put her jeweled crown into the sky as a constellation so she would never be forgotten.

Theseus, in his grief at having lost Ariadne, again forgot to hoist the white sail. When King Aegeus saw the black-sailed ship returning from Crete, he threw himself into the sea in despair.

Theseus inherited his father's throne and he and all of Athens mourned the loss of the old king and in his honor named the sea in which he had drowned the Aegean.

King Minos was beside himself with fury when he discovered that his daughter had fled with the Athenians. He knew that no one but the brilliant Daedalus could have helped Theseus unravel the mystery of the labyrinth, so Daedalus was kept a prisoner in the palace and treated very harshly. Daedalus could not bear to be locked up and let his talents go to waste. Secretly he made two sets of wings, one pair for himself and one pair for his son, Icarus. They were cleverly fashioned of feathers set in beeswax. He showed his son how to use them and warned him not to fly too high or the heat of the sun would melt the wax. Then he led him up to the highest tower, and, flapping their wings, they flew off like two birds. Neither King Minos nor Talos, the robot, could stop their flight.

153

Young and foolish, Icarus could not resist the temptation to rise ever higher into the sky; the whole world seemed at his feet. He flew too close to the sun and the wax began to melt. The feathers came loose, the wings fell apart, and Icarus plunged into the sea and drowned. Sadly Daedalus flew on alone and came to the island of Sicily. His fame had flown ahead of him and the King of Sicily welcomed him warmly, for he too wanted a splendid palace and bathrooms with running water.

As soon as King Minos' ships were mended, he set off in pursuit of Daedalus, the cunning craftsman. He sailed east and he sailed west, and when he came to the Sicilian shore and saw the wondrous palace going up, he had no doubts who was building it. But the king of Sicily hid Daedalus and denied that he had him in his service. Slyly King Minos sent a conch shell up to the palace, with a message that, if anyone could pull a thread through the windings of the conch, he would give him a sack of gold as a reward. The King of Sicily asked Daedalus to solve the problem. Daedalus thought for a while, then he tied a silken thread to an ant, put the ant at one end of the conch shell and a bit of honey at the other end. The ant smelled the honey and found its way through the conch, pulling the thread along with it. When King Minos saw this, he demanded the immediate surrender of Daedalus, for now he had proof that the King of Sicily was hiding him. Nobody but Daedalus could have threaded the conch!

The King of Sicily had to give in. He invited Minos to a feast, promising to surrender Daedalus. As was the custom, King Minos took a bath before the feast. But when he stepped into the fabulous bath that Daedalus had built, boiling water rushed out of the tap and scalded him to death. And Daedalus remained for the rest of his life at the court of the King of Sicily.

After the death of King Minos there was peace between Crete and Athens, and Theseus married Phaedra, Ariadne's younger sister. He became the greatest king Athens ever had, and his fame as a hero spread all over Greece. Another great hero, Pirithoüs, King of the Lapith people in northern Greece, was his inseparable friend. The first time the two heroes had met, they faced each other in combat. But each was so impressed by the other that instead of fighting, they dropped their weapons and swore eternal friendship. Together they performed many great deeds, and when Pirithoüs married a Lapith princess, Theseus, of course, was invited to the wedding feast. The centaurs were invited too, for though wild and lawless they were nonetheless distant relatives. At first they behaved quite mannerly, but as the wine jugs were passed around, they became boisterous and rowdy. Suddenly a young centaur sprang up, grasped the bride by the hair, and galloped away with her. At that, the other centaurs each grasped a screaming girl and took to the hills.

Theseus and Pirithoüs with their men set off in swift pursuit and soon caught up with the centaurs. There was a brutal battle, for the wild centaurs tore up big trees and swung them as clubs. But in Theseus and

Pirithoüs they had found their masters. They were chased out of Greece, and the victorious heroes, with the bride and the other Lapith girls, returned to the feast.

Pirithoüs lived happily for a while, then he became a widower and asked his friend Theseus to help him win a new bride. Theseus vowed to help him, but shuddered when he heard that Pirithoüs wanted no one less than Persephone, the queen of the dead. She was unhappy with Hades, he said. Since Theseus had promised to help his friend, and a promise could not be broken, he descended to the underworld with Pirithoüs. They forced their way past Cerberus and entered the gloomy palace. Hades glowered at the two heroes, who had dared to enter his realm, but he listened politely while they stated their errand. "Sit down on that bench," he said, "so we can discuss the matter." Grim Hades smiled as the two friends sat down, for it was a magic bench from which no one could ever rise. There they were to sit forever with ghosts and bats flitting about their heads.

A long time later Heracles came to Hades on an errand, and pitied the two heroes trying vainly to get up from the bench. He took hold of Theseus and tore him loose with a mighty tug. But when he tried to free Pirithoüs there came a loud earthquake. The gods did not allow Heracles to set him free, for he had shown too great irreverence by daring to want a goddess for a wife. Theseus returned to Athens wiser but thinner, for a part of him had remained stuck to the bench. Ever since, the Athenians have had lean thighs.

157

OEDIPUS

ONE DAY a blind old man came to Theseus and asked for permission to stay in his kingdom and die in peace. No one dared let him stay in their country, for he was pursued by the avenging furies, the Erinyes. Homeless he wandered about. The old man, whose name was Oedipus, then told Theseus his sad story.

His misfortunes had started before he was born. His father, King Laius of Thebes, had been told by the oracle of Delphi that the child his queen, Jocasta, was carrying was fated to kill his father and marry his mother. This must never happen, thought the king, so when Oedipus was born he ordered a servant to take the child away and abandon him in the mountains. But destiny had willed it differently. A shepherd from the neighboring kingdom of Corinth heard the child's cries. He picked up the little boy and carried him to his king. The King and Queen of Corinth were childless and happily they adopted the handsome little boy. They loved him dearly and he never knew that he was not their real son. Without a care in the world he grew to manhood, and one day went to Delphi to find what the future had in store for him. Great was his horror when he heard the words of the oracle! He was destined to kill his father and marry his mother.

This must never happen, thought Oedipus. He took destiny in his own hands and fled across the mountains, never to see his dear parents again.

On a narrow mountain path, he met the chariot of a haughty lord. "Give way for our master's chariot," shouted the servants, and tried to push Oedipus off the path. Angrily Oedipus fought back and in the struggle the lord and all his servants were killed, except for one who escaped. Oedipus continued on his way and came to the city of Thebes. But its seven gates were closed. Nobody dared to enter or leave, for a monster, the Sphinx, had settled on a cliff just outside the city wall. This winged monster with a woman's head and a lion's body challenged all who passed by to solve her riddle. If they couldn't, she tore them to pieces. Nobody yet had solved the riddle of the Sphinx.

"What creature is it that walks on four feet in the morning, on two at noon, and on three in the evening," she asked with a sinister leer when she saw Oedipus.

"It is man," Oedipus answered. "As a child he crawls on four. When grown, he walks upright on his two feet, and in old age he leans on a staff."

The Sphinx let out a horrible scream. Her riddle was solved and she had lost her powers. In despair she threw herself to her death. The gates of Thebes burst open and the people crowded out to thank the stranger who had freed them. Their old king had recently been killed, leaving no son to inherit the throne and when they heard that Oedipus was a prince from Corinth, they asked him to marry their widowed queen and become their king. To be sure, Queen Jocasta was much older than Oedipus, but she was still beautiful, for she wore a magic necklace that the gods had given Harmonia, the first Queen of Thebes. Those who wore that necklace stayed young and beautiful all their lives. Thus Oedipus became King of Thebes, and he ruled the city justly and wisely for many years.

One day the news reached him that the King of Corinth had died the peaceful death of old age, and while he mourned his father, he was glad that he had been spared from a terrible destiny. Shortly afterward, a pestilence broke out in Thebes and people died in great numbers. Oedipus sent for a seer and asked how he could save his people. The pestilence would last until the death of the old king had been avenged, said the seer. Oedipus swore that he would find the man who had killed the old king, and put out his eyes. He sent his men to search till they found the one surviving servant of King Laius' party. When he was brought before King Oedipus, the servant recognized him at once as the slayer of the old king! And now the whole terrible truth came out, for he was also the selfsame servant who had abandoned the infant Oedipus in the mountains, and had known all the while that the child had been found and adopted by the King of Corinth.

In despair Queen Jocasta went to her room and took her own life and Oedipus in horror put out his own eyes and left Thebes, a broken old man. His daughter Antigone went with him, and they wandered from place to place, turned away from every city, till, at last, they came to Athens.

"Not cursed but blessed will be the place where you lie down and close your eyes," said Theseus when he had heard the story. "No man could have tried harder than you to escape his destiny."

The avenging Erinyes, who had been chasing him, now dropped their whips, and Oedipus could die in peace.

His two sons, Eteocles and Polynices, had no regard for the sufferings of their father. They stayed in Thebes and fought over the throne. At last they agreed to take turns being king, one year at a time. Eteocles ruled Thebes first, and when his year was up he refused to give up the throne.

Polynices left Thebes in a rage, taking with him the magic necklace of Harmonia, vowing to return with an army and take his rightful throne by force.

He went to his father-in-law, the King of Argos, and tried to persuade him to send an army to Thebes. The king had an aging and very vain sister who had great influence over him. Polynices promised her the magic necklace of Harmonia, which would make her young and beautiful again, if she could persuade her brother to go against Thebes. So great are the powers of a vain woman that, not only the King of Argos and his men, but seven armies of brave men set forth with Eteocles to storm the seven gates of Thebes, most of them never to return.

Neither could the seven armies storm the seven gates of Thebes, nor could the Thebans drive the attackers away. So it was decided that the two brothers should fight in single combat, the winner to be king.

Eteocles gave his brother a mortal wound, but Polynices, before he fell, dealt him a deadly blow in return. Side by side they lay dead on the field, and all the bloodshed had been in vain.

161

The son of Eteocles became King of Thebes, and Harmonia's necklace, which had brought so much misfortune, was hung up in a temple in Delphi, so no woman would ever wear it again.

THE GOLDEN FLEECE

THE MUSES SANG about handsome Jason and his quest for the Golden Fleece.

Jason of Iolcus was as strong and well bred as he was handsome, for he had been raised by the wise centaur Chiron. Jason's father had brought the boy to the centaur and had asked him to bring him up, for he feared that his own brother, Pelias, who had taken from him the throne of Iolcus, might harm his heir. In Chiron's lonely mountain cave young Jason was raised to be a hero, skilled in all manly sports. When he was grown he left his foster father to go to Iolcus and reclaim his father's throne.

Hera, who was paying a visit to earth, saw the handsome youth as he walked down from the mountain. His golden hair hung to his shoulders and his strong body was wrapped in a leopard skin. Hera was taken by his fine looks. She quickly changed herself into an old crone and stood helplessly at the brink of a swollen stream as if she did not dare to wade across. Jason offered politely to carry her and lifted her on his strong shoulders. He started to wade and at first she was very light. But with each step she grew heavier, and when he reached midstream, she was so heavy that his feet sank deep into the mud. He lost one of his sandals, but struggled bravely on, and when he reached the other side, the old crone revealed herself as the goddess Hera.

"Lo," she said. "You are a mortal after my liking, I shall stand by you and help you win back your throne from your uncle Pelias." This was a promise the goddess gladly gave, for she had a grudge against Pelias, who had once forgotten to include her when he sacrificed to the gods.

Jason thanked her and went on his way in high spirits. When he arrived in Iolcus, people crowded around him, wondering who the handsome stranger might be, but when King Pelias saw him, his cheeks paled. An oracle had predicted that a youth with only one sandal would be his undoing. Pelias feigned great friendship when Jason said who he was and why he had come, but underneath he held dark thoughts and planned to do away with his guest. Pelias feasted Jason and flattered him and promised him the throne as soon as he had performed a heroic deed to prove himself worthy of being a king.

"In the kingdom of Colchis, at the shores of the Black Sea," said Pelias, "on a branch in a dark grove, there hangs a golden fleece shining as brightly as the sun. Bring the fleece to me and the throne shall be yours."

The Golden Fleece was once the coat of a flying ram, sent by Zeus to save the life of young Prince Phrixus of Thessaly. The crops had failed and Phrixus' evil stepmother had convinced his father that he must sacrifice his son to save his country from famine. Sadly the king built an altar and put his son on it, but Zeus hated human sacrifice, and as the king lifted his knife, a golden ram swooped down from the skies and flew off with Phrixus on his back. They flew far to the east and landed in the kingdom of Colchis. The King of Colchis understood that Phrixus had been sent by the gods. He gave him his daughter in marriage and sacrificed the ram. Its glittering fleece was hung in a sacred grove and it was the greatest treasure of the country.

King Pelias was certain that Jason would not return alive, for he knew that the warlike king of Colchis would not part with the fleece and that a never-sleeping dragon was guarding it. But Pelias did not know that Jason had Hera's help.

"Give me timber and men to build for me a sturdy ship and I shall sail off at once," said Jason. The king gave him what he asked for and a

great ship, the *Argo,* was built. It was the most seaworthy ship ever seen. Athena, herself prodded by Hera, put a piece of sacred oak in its prow. The oak had the power to speak in time of danger and advise Jason what to do.

With a ship like that it was not hard for Jason to gather a crew of heroes. Even Heracles came with his young friend Hylas. Calaïs and Zetes, winged sons of the North Wind, joined, and Orpheus came along to inspire the crew with his music. Soon each of the fifty oars of the ship was manned by a hero who swore to stand by Jason through all dangers.

Before they set sail, the heroes who called themselves the Argonauts, sacrificed richly to the gods and made sure to forget no one. Poseidon was in a good mood. He called for the West Wind and under full sail the *Argo* sped toward the east. When the wind grew tired and died down, the Argonauts put out their oars and rowed with all their might. Orpheus beat out the time with his lyre and the ship cut through the waves like an arrow. One after the other the heroes grew tired and pulled in their oars. Only Heracles and Jason were left rowing, each trying to outlast the other. Jason finally fainted, but just as he slumped forward, Heracles' huge oar broke in two, so equal glory was won by them both.

The Argonauts landed at a wooded coast so Heracles could cut

164

himself a new oar. While Heracles searched for a suitable tree, his young friend Hylas went to a pool to fill his jar with fresh water. When the nymph of the pool saw the handsome boy bending down, she fell in love with him. She pulled him down with her to the bottom of the pool and Hylas vanished forever without leaving a trace.

Heracles went out of his mind with grief when he could not find his friend. He ran through the woods, calling for Hylas, beating down whatever was in his way. The Argonauts, brave as they were, all feared Heracles when he was struck with folly. They hastily boarded the ship and sailed away without him.

On toward the east the Argonauts sailed until they came to a country ruled by a king who was known for his knowledge and wisdom. They went ashore to ask the way to Colchis, but the king was so weak that he could barely answer their questions. He was so thin that only his skin held his bones together. Whenever food was set before him, three disgusting Harpies, fat birds with women's heads, swooped down and devoured it. What they did not eat they left so foul and filthy that it was not fit to be eaten. No one in his kingdom could keep the Harpies away.

The Argonauts felt sorry for the starving king. They told him to have his table set, and when the Harpies swooped down again, Zetes and

165

Calaïs, the sons of the North Wind, took to their wings. They could fly faster than the Harpies, and when they caught them, they whipped the evil pests so hard that they barely escaped with their lives. The Harpies flew to the south, never to be seen again. At last the famished king could eat in peace. He could not thank the Argonauts enough and told them how to set their course and what dangers they would encounter. No ship had yet been able to reach the shores of Colchis, he said, for the passage to the Black Sea was blocked by two moving rocks. The rocks rolled apart and clashed together, crushing whatever came between them. But if a ship could move as fast as a bird in flight, it might get through. He gave Jason a dove and told him to send the bird ahead of the ship. If the dove came through alive, they had a chance, he said. If not, they had better give up and turn back.

The Argonauts took leave of the king and sailed toward the clashing rocks. From afar they could hear the din and the heroes trembled, but as the rocks rolled apart, Jason released the dove and the bird flew between them like a dart. Only the very tips of its tail feathers were clipped off when the rocks clashed together.

"All men to the oars!" Jason shouted. Orpheus grasped his lyre and played and his music inspired the heroes to row as never before. The *Argo* shot ahead like an arrow when the rocks rolled apart, and only the very end of its stern was crushed as they clashed together. Again the rocks rolled apart and stood firmly anchored. The spell was broken, and from then on ships could safely sail in and out of the Black Sea.

The Black Sea was a dangerous sea to sail upon, and Hera had her hands full, guiding the Argonauts through perils. But with her help Jason brought his ship safely through raging storms, past pirate shores and cannibal island, and the Argonauts finally arrived in Colchis.

Aeëtes, King of Colchis, a son of Helios, the sun, was a very inhospitable king. In fact he was so inhospitable that he killed all foreigners who came to his country. When he saw the *Argo* landing he was furious, and when Jason led his men to his palace and said that they were all great heroes and had come to offer the king their services in return for the Golden Fleece, he fumed with rage. "Very well," he said to Jason. "Tomorrow, between sunrise and sunset, you must harness my fire-breathing bulls, plow up a field, and sow it with dragon's teeth as Cad-

mus did at Thebes. If you succeed, the Golden Fleece is yours. But if you fail, I shall cut out the tongues and lop off the hands of you and all your great heroes." King Aeëtes knew well that no man could withstand the searing heat that blew from the bulls' nostrils. What he did not know was that Hera was helping Jason.

Hera knew that the king's daughter, Medea, who stood at her father's side with modestly downcast eyes, was the only one who could save Jason. She was a lovely young sorceress, a priestess of the witch-goddess Hecate, and must be made to fall in love with Jason. So Hera asked Aphrodite to send her little son Eros to shoot one of his arrows of love into Medea's heart. Aphrodite promised Eros a beautiful enamel ball, and he shot an arrow into Medea's heart just as she lifted up her eyes and saw Jason. Her golden eyes gleamed; never had she seen anyone so handsome. She just had to use her magic and save him from her cruel father; there was nothing she would not do to save Jason's life. She went to Hecate's temple and implored the witch-goddess to help her and, guided by the witch-goddess, she concocted a magic salve so powerful that for one day neither iron nor fire could harm the one who was covered with it.

In the dark of the night, Medea sent for Jason. When he came to the temple, she blushingly told him that she loved him so much she would betray her own father to save him. She gave him the magic salve and told him to go up to the fire-breathing bulls without fear. Jason took the young sorceress in his arms and swore by all the gods of Olympus to make her his queen and love her to his dying day. Hera heard him and nodded, very pleased.

When the sun rose in the morning, Jason went straight up to the fire-breathing bulls. They bellowed and belched flames at him, but with Medea's salve he was invulnerable and so strong that he harnessed the bulls and drove them back and forth till the whole field was plowed. Then he seeded the dragon's teeth, and right away a host of warriors sprang up from the furrows. As Cadmus had done, he threw a rock among them and watched from afar as they killed one another. Before the sun had set, they all lay dead.

168

Jason had fulfilled his task, but King Aeëtes had no intention of keeping his part of the bargain. He called his men together and ordered them to seize the *Argo* and kill the foreigners at daybreak. In secrecy,

Medea went to Jason and told him that he must take the Golden Fleece, now rightfully his, and flee from Colchis before dawn. Under cover of night she led him to the dark grove where the Golden Fleece, shining like the sun, hung on a branch of a tree. Around the trunk of the tree lay coiled the never-sleeping dragon. But Medea chanted incantations and bewitched the dragon. She stared at it with her golden eyes and it fell into a deep magic sleep. Quickly Jason took the Golden Fleece and ran with Medea to the waiting *Argo,* and quietly they slipped out to sea.

At daybreak, when the king's men were to attack the ship, they found it was gone. So were the Golden Fleece and the king's daughter, Medea. Red-faced with fury, Aeëtes set off in pursuit with his great fleet of Colchian warships. He wanted the Golden Fleece back and he wanted to punish his daughter. The fastest of his ships, steered by one of his sons, soon overtook the *Argo.*

The Argonauts thought themselves lost, but again Medea saved them.

She called to her brother, who stood at the helm of his ship, and pretended to be sorry for what she had done. She said she would go home with him if he would meet her alone on a nearby island. At the same time, she whispered to Jason to lie in wait and kill her brother when he came. She knew that her father would have to stop the pursuit to give his son a funeral.

Hera and all the gods looked in horror at Medea, stained with her brother's blood. No mortal could commit a worse crime than to cause the death of his own kin. Zeus in anger threw thunderbolts. Lightning flashed, thunder roared, and the sea foamed. Then the sacred piece of oak in the bow of the *Argo* spoke. "Woe," it said, "woe to you all. Not a one among you will reach Greece unless the great sorceress Circe consents to purify Medea and Jason of their sin."

Tossed about by howling winds and towering waves, the Argonauts sailed in search of Circe's dwelling. At long last, off the coast of Italy, they found her palace. Medea warned the Argonauts not to leave the ship, for Circe was a dangerous sorceress who amused herself by changing men who came to her island into the animal nearest the nature of each man. Some became lions, some rabbits, but most of them were changed into pigs and asses. Medea took Jason by the hand so no harm would befall him, and went ashore.

Circe was Medea's aunt. Like all the descendants of Helios, the sun, she had a golden glint in her eyes, and the moment she saw Medea, she recognized her as her kin. But she was not happy to see her niece, for through her magic she knew what Medea had done. Still she consented to sacrifice to Zeus and ask him to forgive Medea and Jason for their crime. The scented smoke of her burnt offering of sweetmeats and cakes reached Zeus and put him in a good humor. He listened to Circe's words and again smiled down upon Medea and Jason.

They thanked Circe and rushed back to the ship. The Argonauts rejoiced. Now they could set sail for Greece. But still they had to pass through dangerous and bewitched waters. Soon they came to the island of the Sirens. The Sirens were half birds, half women, not loathsome like the Harpies, but enchanting creatures. They sat on a cliff, half hidden by sea spray, and sang so beautifully that all sailors who heard them dived into the sea and tried to swim to them, only to drown or pine to death at the Sirens' feet. When the alluring voices of the Sirens reached the ears

of the Argonauts, Orpheus grasped his lyre and sang so loudly and
sweetly that all other sounds were drowned out, and not one of the Argonauts jumped overboard.

After a while the *Argo* had to sail through a narrow strait that was
guarded by two monsters. On one side lurked the monster Scylla. From
her waist up she looked like a woman, but instead of legs, six furious,
snarling dogs grew out from her hips, and they tore to pieces whatever
came close to them. The monster Charybdis lived on the other side of the
strait. She was forever hungry and sucked into her gullet all ships that
ventured within her reach.

Helplessly, the *Argo* drifted between the two monsters, and the
Argonauts again gave themselves up for lost, when up from the bottom
of the sea rose the playful Nereids. They had come at Hera's bidding
and they lifted up the *Argo* and threw it from hand to hand over the dangerous waters until it reached the open sea beyond. Poseidon called for
the West Wind and the *Argo* sped homeward under full sail.

173

A loud cheer rang out from the valiant crew when they sighted the shore of Greece. They had been away for many long years and were homesick. But as the *Argo* neared the port of Iolcus, the ship was hailed by a fisherman who warned Jason that King Pelias had heard of his safe return and had made plans to kill him. Jason was downcast at his uncle's treachery, but Medea, her eyes flashing, asked to be set ashore alone. Once again she wanted to save his life.

Disguised as an old witch, she entered Iolcus, saying that she had magic herbs to sell that would make old creatures young again. The people crowded around her, wondering from where the witch had come. King Pelias himself came out from his palace and asked her to prove that what she said was true, for he felt he was growing old.

"Bring me the oldest ram in your flock and I will show you the magic of my herbs," said Medea.

An old ram was brought to her and she put it into a caldron full of water. On top she sprinkled some of her magic herbs, and lo! the water in the caldron boiled and out of the steam and bubbles sprang a frisky young lamb.

Now King Pelias asked Medea to make him young too. She answered that only his daughters could do that, but she would gladly sell them her magic herbs. But the herbs she gave them had no magic at all, and so King Pelias found his death in the boiling caldron at his own daughters' hands.

Now the throne of Iolcus was Jason's, but again Medea had committed a terrible crime. She had tricked innocent daughters into killing their own father. The gods turned from her and she changed from a lovely young sorceress into an evil witch. The people of Iolcus refused to accept her for their queen and took another king in Jason's stead. With the loss of his throne, Jason also lost his love for Medea. He forgot that he had sworn to love her till his dying day and that she had committed her crimes for his sake. He asked her to leave so he could marry the Princess of Corinth and inherit her father's kingdom.

Medea, scorned and furious, turned more and more to evil sorcery. To revenge herself on Jason, she sent a magic robe to his new bride. It was a beautiful gown, but the moment the bride put it on she went up in flames and so did the whole palace. Then Medea disappeared into a dark cloud, riding in a carriage drawn by two dragons.

174

Jason found no more happiness, for when he broke his sacred oath to Medea, he lost Hera's good will. His good looks left him and so did his luck and his friends. Lonesome and forgotten, he sat one day in the shade of his once glorious ship, the *Argo,* now rotting on the beach of Corinth. Suddenly the sacred piece of oak in the prow broke off, fell on him, and killed him.

The Golden Fleece was hung in Apollo's temple in Delphi, a wonder for all Greeks to behold and a reminder of the great deeds of Jason and the Argonauts.

THE CALYDONIAN BOAR HUNT

MELEAGER of Calydonia was one of the heroes who had sailed with Jason on the *Argo*. No one could throw a spear with greater skill than he. Still he was powerless to stop a fearful boar that was ravaging his father's kingdom. The king, one day, had forgotten to include Artemis when he sacrificed to the gods, and in revenge the angry goddess sent the biggest boar ever seen. The boar had tusks as big as an elephant's and bristles as sharp as steel. Meleager sent for the Argonauts and all the great athletes of Greece and asked them to come to Calydonia and hunt down the monstrous beast. Great glory awaited the one who could destroy the Calydonian Boar.

176

Many heroes came to the hunt, and also a girl whose name was Atalanta. She was the fastest runner in Greece and a great huntress as well. When some of the men grumbled at hunting with a girl, Meleager ruled that a girl who could outrun them all would certainly be welcome to join the chase. Still grumbling, the men had to give in.

For days the heroes feasted at the Calydonian court. Then they offered rich sacrifices to the gods and went off to the hunt. They drove the boar out of its lair, and as it charged, spears and arrows flew wild. When the dust settled, seven men lay dead, some killed by the boar, some by the arrows of their excited companions. Atalanta alone kept a cool head. She ran swiftly hither and thither till she could take good aim, and then she let an arrow fly. The arrow stopped the boar just in time to save the life of a hero who had stumbled in front of the onrushing beast. Quickly Meleager leaped forward and hurled his spear with all his might. The beast rolled over and lay dead.

Meleager offered the hide and the tusks to Atalanta. These trophies were hers, he said, for it was she who stopped the boar. Again the men protested, for it hurt their pride to see a girl walk off with all the glory. Meleager's two uncles teased him and said that he must be in love with the girl. "Just wait till your wife finds out about this!" they said, smiling maliciously.

In a rage Meleager hurled his spear at his taunting uncles, killing them both. When Meleager's mother heard that her son had slain her two brothers, she, too, flew into a rage. She ran to her treasure chest and took out a half-charred log. It was a magic log that held Meleager's life.

This log had been burning in the hearth when Meleager was born. The three Fates had come to see the infant, and the mother had overheard them say it was a pity that the handsome child would die as soon as the log had burned up. Quickly the mother had seized the log, beaten out the flames, and had hidden it among her dearest treasures. Thus Meleager had lived to become a great hero.

Now in her fury, the queen flung the old dry log into the fire. As it burst into flames and was consumed, Meleager felt a searing pain shoot through his body and fell dead.

177

The Calydonian Boar Hunt, which had begun with a feast, ended with a funeral. Only Atalanta was happy. She had won her trophies in competition with the greatest heroes of Greece.

THE APPLES OF LOVE AND
THE APPLE OF DISCORD

ATALANTA, like Artemis, loved no men, though many men fell in love with her because she was so graceful when she ran.

When she was born her father had cruelly abandoned her in the wilderness, for he had hoped for a son. But she did not perish, for a she-bear heard her cries and carried her gently to her den, nursed her, and raised her with her cubs.

Years later, an astonished huntsman saw a girl racing with wild beasts through the woods. He caught her in a snare and brought her home with him. Soon she learned to talk and act like a human, and her foster father was very proud of her fleetness of foot. He took her to athletic games and she won all the races. Her fame spread over Greece, and now her real father proudly reclaimed her as his long-lost daughter. He was a king and a king's daughter could not be allowed to run about unmarried, so he began to search for a suitable husband for her. But Atalanta did not want a husband. To be left in peace, she said she would only marry a man who could beat her in a running race. However, anyone who raced her and lost would forfeit his life. That would scare all suitors away, she thought. But she was so lovely that many suitors tried their luck anyway and they all lost their lives.

One day a young prince whose name was Melanion came to court her. He was smarter than the others. He knew that he could not outrun

Atalanta, so he sacrificed to Aphrodite and prayed for her help. The goddess of love, who wanted to see all pretty girls married, gave Melanion three golden apples and told him what to do.

When the race began, Atalanta, certain that she would win, let Melanion have a head start. When she caught up with him, Melanion threw a golden apple at her feet. It glittered so beautifully that she had to stop and pick it up. Soon she overtook him again and Melanion threw the second apple, this time a bit farther away. She left the track and made a dash for the apple. When again Melanion heard her light footsteps behind him, he threw the third apple far into the bushes. Atalanta just had to have that one too, and before she found it, Melanion had crossed the finish line. So he had won her and they were married and Atalanta treasured her golden apples and loved her clever husband dearly. They lived happily for many years and never forgot to honor Aphrodite, who had brought them together. But they did not show proper respect to Zeus and he changed them into a pair of lions for punishment. For the rest of their lives they ran as lions hunting side by side through the woods.

Peleus, a young king of Thessaly, had Atalanta to thank for his life, for it was he who had stumbled in front of the Calydonian Boar when she stopped it with her arrow. He had also been one of the Argonauts and was one of the greatest athletes in Greece, a favorite of the gods. Zeus gave him a beautiful Nereid, Thetis, for his bride, and all the gods came to the wedding. Only Eris, the spirit of strife, had not been invited. She was furious, and while everybody was making merry she threw a golden apple among the guests and shouted, "The fairest of the goddesses shall have it!"

Hera, Aphrodite, and Athena rushed to pick it up, each one thinking herself the fairest. It was not a golden apple of love that Eris had thrown, but the apple of discord, and the three goddesses began to quarrel about who should have it. The wedding broke up on a sour note, and in heated dispute the goddesses retired to high Olympus.

Thetis, the bride, was not happy at being married to a mortal, for her children would not be immortal, as she was. No god had dared to marry her, for an oracle had predicted that she would bear her husband a son who would become greater than his father. Peleus, of course, thought himself the most fortunate of men.

In time, Thetis bore her husband many children. Trying to make

179

them immortal, she held them over sacred fire to burn away their mortality, but none survived the ordeal. At last, she gave birth to a boy sturdier than the others. He withstood the fire, and she had almost succeeded in making him immortal, when Peleus rushed into her room and snatched the child away. Thetis was so hurt and disappointed that she went back to the sea and never returned. The little boy was brought up by Chiron, the wise centaur, and he grew to be the greatest warrior that Greece has ever known. He was invulnerable except for his heel by which his mother held him over the fire. His name was Achilles.

Meanwhile discord reigned on Olympus. The three goddesses quarreled on, and none of the gods dared to say which of them was the fairest.

One day as Zeus looked down on earth, his eyes fell on Paris, a prince of Troy. He was overwhelmingly handsome, as were most men in the royal house of Troy. His grand-uncle Ganymede was such a good-looking boy that Zeus, in the shape of an eagle, had stolen him from his father and carried him to Olympus to be his cupbearer. Anchises, another relative of Paris, was so exceedingly handsome that Aphrodite herself fell in love with him. She took on the shape of a princess so she could marry him and bore him a son whose name was Aeneas.

But Paris outshone all his relatives, and someone as handsome as he must be the best judge of beauty, thought Zeus. He told Hermes to lead the three goddesses down to Mount Ida near Troy, where Paris was herding the royal sheep and cows, and let Paris judge between them.

Paris stared in speechless wonder when the three radiant goddesses appeared before him. Hermes gave him the golden apple and told him to award it to the most beautiful of them.

"Give it to me," said white-armed Hera, "and all of Asia shall be your kingdom."

"Choose me," said gray-eyed Athena, "and you shall be the wisest of men."

"The most beautiful woman on earth shall be yours if you give me the apple," said Aphrodite.

Paris was young and loved beauty more than power or wisdom, and so he gave the apple to Aphrodite.

180

Aphrodite happily took the golden apple, and did not give it a thought that the most beautiful woman on earth, Helen, Queen of Sparta, already had a husband.

LOVELY was the song of the Muses about the great beauty of Helen of Troy. She was a daughter of Zeus and her beauty had been a wonder to all from the time she was born. Zeus in the disguise of a swan had flown down from Olympus to court her mother, Leda, and Leda had laid two blue eggs. When the eggs were hatched, Helen and her brother, Pollux, came out from one of them. They were the children of Zeus and immortal. From the other egg came their half sister and brother, Clytemnestra and Castor, children of Leda's mortal husband, King Tyndareus.

Castor and Pollux were inseparable from the time they were born, and both grew up to be great athletes. Castor won fame as a tamer of horses, Pollux as a boxer. They protected each other to the last breath. When side by side they fell in battle, Pollux went to Olympus, while Castor, being mortal, was sent to Hades. They missed each other so much that Zeus took pity on them. He allowed Pollux to give his brother half of his immortality and from then on the Heavenly Twins always stayed together, half the time on Olympus, the other half in Hades' realm.

The two sisters, Helen and Clytemnestra, grew up at the court of their mortal father, King Tyndareus. Clytemnestra soon was given in marriage to Agamemnon, the great King of Mycenae. But Helen had so many suitors that Tyndareus did not know whom to choose. He feared that if he gave her hand to one the crowd of rejected suitors would fall upon him. His palace was besieged by Helen's admirers and ever more came. Among them was Odysseus, a wise young prince. When he saw all

182

the suitors, he withdrew his proposal, for he knew that there would always be fighting over a woman as lovely as Helen. Instead he asked for the hand of her gentle cousin, Penelope, and he advised King Tyndareus how to solve his problem. He must ask all the suitors to accept the one he chose for Helen's husband and swear to stand by and help to win her back should anyone try to steal her. The suitors agreed. Each one hoped that the choice would fall on him, and they all took the oath. Tyndareus then gave Helen's hand to Menelaus of Sparta, and all the other suitors left without grumbling.

Helen had been the Queen of Sparta for many happy years and her fame as the most beautiful woman on earth had spread all over, when Aphrodite promised her to Paris. The Trojans begged Paris to forget Aphrodite's promise, or a terrible misfortune would surely befall them. But Paris ignored their warnings and sailed across the Aegean Sea, to steal Helen from King Menelaus and bring her back to Troy.

Helen sat serene and happy, surrounded by her ladies, weaving and sewing her finest wools, when Paris entered the palace in Sparta. Just as she looked up and saw him, Eros shot an arrow of love into her heart. She gathered her treasures without hesitation and eloped with him for Troy.

A brisk wind carried them out to sea, but before they had sailed far, the wine-dark waters grew glassy and calm, and Nereus, the kind old man of the sea, rose from the depths. He warned them to return or dire woe would befall them and their kin. But Helen and Paris had eyes and ears only for each other and did not hear his warning.

They landed in Troy and the Trojans received her with great joy, proud that the most beautiful woman on earth was now Helen of Troy.

But Menelaus was not a man to stand idly by, whether or not his queen had been promised to Paris by a goddess. He reminded Helen's old suitors of their oath. They joined him with all their warriors, and it was not long before a huge Greek fleet arrived in Troy to fetch Helen back to Sparta. The Trojans refused to give Helen up, and Troy was hard to conquer, for it was surrounded by a high wall built by Apollo and Poseidon. After long talks, it was decided that Paris and Menelaus should fight in single combat and Helen would go to the winner. Paris was no warrior. He preferred to rest on silken pillows and gaze into Helen's beautiful eyes. But Aphrodite came to his rescue and hid him in a cloud and since

Menelaus could not find his opponent, the duel was undecided. Then the two armies clashed together.

For ten long years, the Greeks and the Trojans fought over Helen. The gods watched with great interest and even took part in the fighting themselves. Hera, angry with Paris for not giving the apple to her, fought for the Greeks. Wise and just Athena was also annoyed with Paris, so even though she was protectress of Troy, she fought for the Greeks. Ares fought wherever the battle was hottest, and when he himself was wounded, he frightened both armies with his howls. Sweet Aphrodite herself entered the raging battle to help her darling Paris and she also was wounded. "Enough!" called Zeus, and he ordered all the gods to withdraw from the battle. They sat on the walls of Troy and watched the mortals decide the outcome for themselves.

Many great heroes fell on both sides, but the Greeks could not storm the mighty walls of Troy and the Trojans could not put the Greeks to flight as long as Achilles, the invulnerable son of Thetis, fought for them. Though Paris was no great marksman, fate had chosen him to slay the great hero Achilles. Apollo, unseen by the other gods, ran to Paris's side and guided his hand as he drew taut his bow. The arrow struck Achilles in the heel, his only vulnerable spot. Mortally wounded, he fell to the ground. The Greeks mourned greatly the loss of their hero Achilles, and took their revenge on Paris. He fell, pierced by one of the poisoned arrows that Heracles had given to Philoctetes.

Shortly afterward, the Greeks broke camp, boarded their ships, and sailed away. They left on the shore a large wooden horse. The Trojans thought they had finally routed the Greeks, and in triumph, they pulled the horse into their city as a trophy. But the horse was hollow and filled with Greek warriors. In the dark of the night, they crept out and opened wide the city gates. The wily Greeks had not left, but had been hiding behind an island. Now they came pouring into the city and proud Troy was destroyed.

Helen was brought back to Sparta in triumph to sit among her ladies as lovely as ever, embroidering in lavender and purple threads on the finest wools.

184

Of the royal house of Troy no one but Aphrodite's son Aeneas, his father, and his young son remained. The goddess returned to take them out of the smoking ruins and lead them to safety.

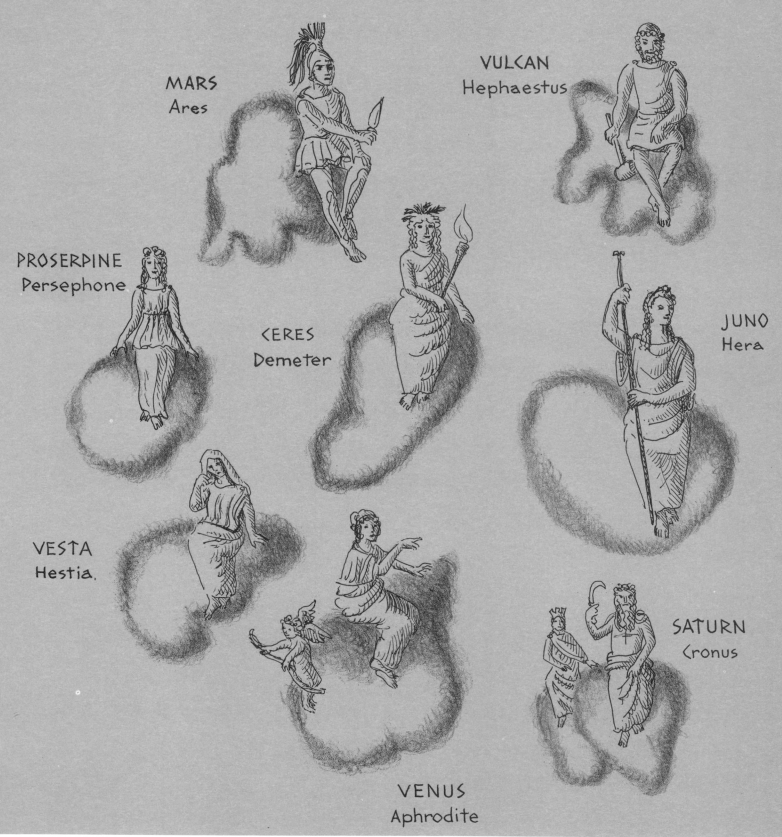

MARS
Ares

VULCAN
Hephaestus

PROSERPINE
Persephone

CERES
Demeter

JUNO
Hera

VESTA
Hestia

SATURN
Cronus

VENUS
Aphrodite

186   Aeneas wandered from land to land, till at last he came to Italy, where he founded a kingdom. The gods looked on him with favor, for it was fated that his descendants should build the mighty city of Rome.

So it came to pass! The Romans built huge temples to the Olym-

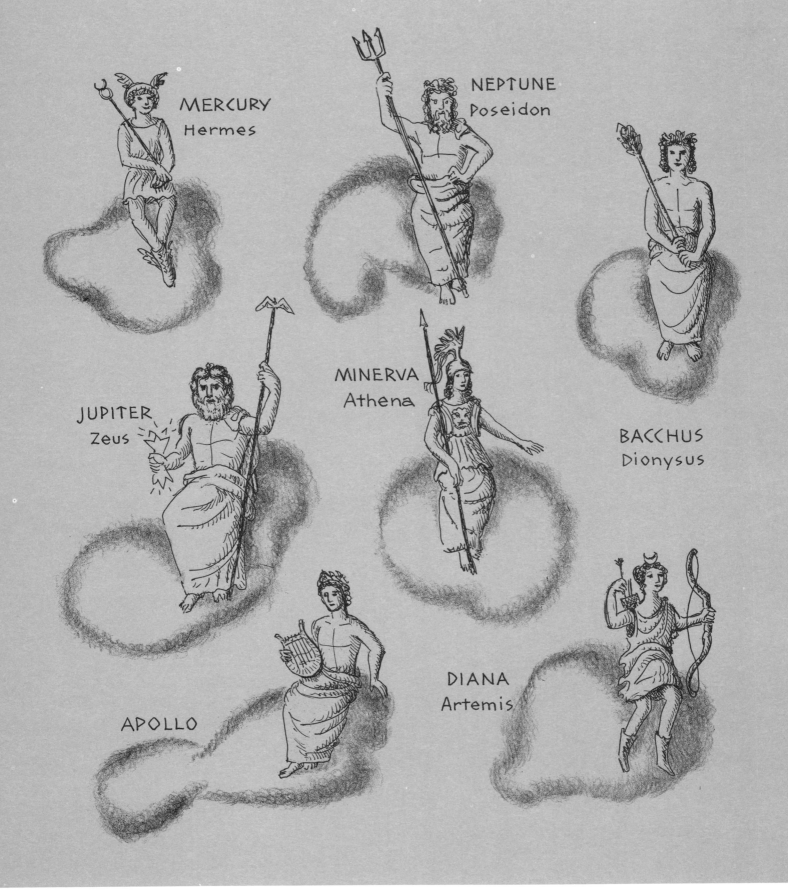

MERCURY
Hermes

NEPTUNE
Poseidon

JUPITER
Zeus

MINERVA
Athena

BACCHUS
Dionysus

APOLLO

DIANA
Artemis

pian gods, not so beautiful as the Greek ones, but much more luxurious, and the glory of the gods became greater than ever. They were given Roman names instead of their Greek ones, but they were still the same gods and it is under their Roman names that we know them best today.

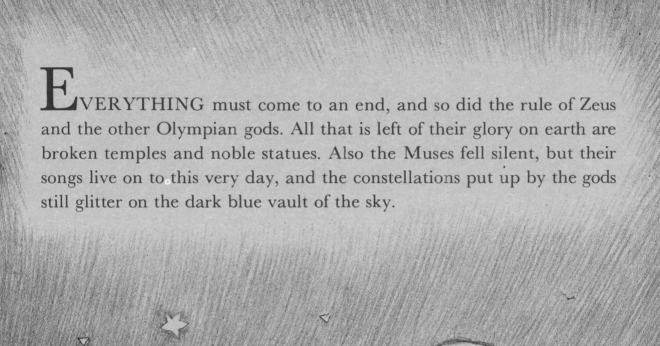

EVERYTHING must come to an end, and so did the rule of Zeus and the other Olympian gods. All that is left of their glory on earth are broken temples and noble statues. Also the Muses fell silent, but their songs live on to this very day, and the constellations put up by the gods still glitter on the dark blue vault of the sky.

INDEX

191

DATE DUE
